Doing Field Research

Doing

Field

Research

John M. Johnson

THE FREE PRESS
A Division of Macmillan Publishing Co., Inc.
NEW YORK

Collier Macmillan Publishers
LONDON

To Suzanne

The Free Press
A Division of Macmillan Publishing Co., Inc.
866 Third Avenue, New York, N.Y.   10022

Collier–Macmillan Canada Ltd.

Library of Congress Catalog Card Number: 74–27599

Printed in the United States of America

printing number

1 2 3 4 5 6 7 8 9 10

Library of Congress Cataloging in Publication Data

Johnson, John M
   Doing field research.

   Includes bibliographical references and index.
   1. Social science--Research. 2. Social sciences--
Field work. 3. Participant observation. 4. Evalua-
tion research (Social action programs)--United States.
I. Title.
H62.J5834   300'.7'2   74-27599
ISBN 0-02-916600-4

Copyright Acknowledgments

Contents

Preface

In the following pages I present a detailed description and analysis of a sociological field-research project. The project involved my investigations of social welfare activities, and took place in five offices of two large metropolitan departments of public welfare. The initial plans for the research began in the fall of 1969, and the major portion of the field observations was undertaken in 1970–71.

I initially intended to give some attention to the field-research process while I pursued my primary interest in welfare activities, with the hope of producing an appendix on field research methods, a convention in sociological field researches. I did not intend to write a book about field-research methods; rather, this work developed out of my experiences as a sociological field worker.

In the social science literature, "participant observation" and "field research" are often used interchangeably. In the broadest sense, these terms refer to a manner of conducting a scientific investigation wherein the observer maintains a face-to-face involvement with the members of a particular social setting for purposes of scientific inquiry. Thus, a field researcher is one who participates with a group of people in order to observe their everyday actions in their natural social settings.

The history of field research is almost as long as the history of the social sciences. The first field researches were the early anthropological investigations of "primitive" cultures done at the turn of the century. The ethnographic descriptions produced by the Chicago School in sociology during the 1920s and 1930s established field research as a legitimate mode of scientific inquiry. Participant observation and field research are often referred to as qualitative, as distinguished from quantitative, methods. Qualitative research affords us an in-depth, detailed, descriptive account of social actions occurring at a specific place and time. Quantitative methods, on the other hand, usually involve statistical measurements of various kinds which are cross-tabulated with one another to explain the variability of social events. All social scientists have recognized the existence of these two distinctive research traditions for many decades.

One distinction between participant observation and field research is drawn in this volume which requires a brief comment. In light of the creative intellectual developments originating from several disciplines during the last decade, I think we are well advised to recognize that, in a very fundamental sense, all modes of scientific research involve participant observation. This is so because it is only our participation as members of society which gives us a mastery of a natural language and a common-sense knowledge of cultural meanings, faculties which are essential in allowing us to make sense of what we observe in our everyday lives. Our mastery of these social competencies is achieved before we set foot in our first class in methodology to learn the techniques of scientific observation. In this light, statistical cross tabulations, experimental research, surveys, and field research are all, in the most basic sense, modes of participant observation. Field research is distinguished from these other forms of participant observation in that it involves inquiries in and of the natural settings of daily life. Further details on the justification for this distinction are presented in Chapter 1.

This book has three main parts. First, the major arguments in the traditional methodological literature about the problems of conducting field research are discussed. Next, the research situations which occurred during my particular field observations in the social welfare offices are described. In this regard, some of the chapters are organized on the basis of what many others have seen as the major problems of field-research conduct. Chapter 3, for example, analyzes the problems of gaining and managing entree to the settings where the research is done. Chapter 4 describes some of the actual methods used in developing personal relationships of trust with the members in the setting. Chapter 5 discusses the problems of personal relationships in field research and their influence on data collection. Finally, Chapter 6 analyzes the intricate fusions of thinking and feeling in social research, and Chapter 7 is concerned with how a research report is put together.

Finally, the book compares the traditional. conceptions of field-research practice and my personal experience within the context of current debates about social science objectivity. My field-research experiences and reflections have led me to a reevaluation of several of the fundamental issues concerning objectivity. While an account of the practice of scientific research can justly be seen as a legitimate goal in itself, I think it is our continuing concern about the objectivity of our social science knowledge which is at the root of our ongoing interest in methods.

We live in an age when those of us who are interested in understanding the nature of contemporary events are virtually inundated with information. It often seems as though we have barely become familiar with the facts of a given problem when we discover that the information has been made obsolete by the rush of events. It is virtually impossible for any one person to be familiar with all of these changing facts about our world. In a situation such as this, it is imperative that we have an understanding of the nature of scientific inquiry that will allow us to process this continuing information flow in some intelligible manner. Long after the reader has forgotten the specific substantive details about the social welfare investigation reported here, I hope that the general perspective on scientific research conduct developed in these pages will remain, to aid the reader in developing this faculty.

There are many individuals to whom I owe a debt of gratitude for assisting me with this effort. Professor Jack Douglas deserves a special note, because his exemplary intellectual commitments inspired my work. I also owe a special debt to my faculty mentors and sponsors, Professors Joseph Gusfield, C. Dale Johnson, Stanford Lyman, and Nicos Mouratides. These men, individually and collectively, embody those attributes I find worthwhile in the practice of sociology.

Between the completion of the original manuscript and its publication by The Free Press, many revisions have been made. I would like to acknowledge the assistance of several colleagues who cared enough to provide their criticism and commentary on the earlier drafts. These include David Altheide, John Anderson, Howard S. Becker, John Bradford, Rochelle Daniels, Jack Douglas, Andrea Fontana, Charles Freeman, John Scott Fuller, John Lofland, Peter Manning, Bernard S. Phillips, Steve Phillips, Ron Ryno, Dennis Stouffer, and Carol Warren. The editorial staff at The Free Press were especially helpful. David A. McDermott was important for his early encouragement of the book. Subsequent editorial assistance by Arthur L. Iamele, Charles E. Smith, and George A. Rowland proved absolutely invaluable in turning my tortured prose into a document which is more or less intelligible.

In addition to the gracious assistance provided by my sociology colleagues, personal friends played important roles in the completion of the project. They provided assistance of all kinds, from financial aid to moral support. Most importantly, however, they were friends. I wish to specifically acknowledge my gratitude to Carla and David Altheide, John Anderson, Elizabeth and

Larrie Brainard, Jeanie and Jon Olson, and Betsy and Dale Pontius.

Words fail to do justice to my feelings of gratitude to my wife, Suzanne. Her love and assistance were essential to the research. Our arguments about dangling modifiers and other matters now seem trivial. I dedicate this book to her, with love.

Finally, I wish to thank all of the social workers who assisted me with the research. In the most basic sense, they were the ones who made the work possible. I feel I learned very much from them, but provided so little in return. I hope this book and the other research reports partially repay my indebtedness to them. I only regret that the original research agreement prohibits me from acknowledging them by name.

An author's expression of gratitude to friends and colleagues is conventionally followed by a statement absolving them of any responsibility for the facts and judgments expressed in the book. This convention is one of the topics analyzed in Chapter 6. Anticipating that discussion, I would add here that I am solely responsible for any grammatical errors in the book, but that those mentioned in the above paragraphs share with me the moral responsibility for the substantive materials.

Chapter 1

Participant Observation, Field Research, and Objectivity in Sociology

THESE ARE TIMES of profound self-doubt for those who practice social science. Challenges to long-accepted truths emanate from many quarters. These challenges involve all aspects of the social sciences: theories, methods, and even the ultimate purposes of social science itself. Scientists have traditionally considered the scientific method of knowing as being "more objective" than any existing alternatives. At the most fundamental level, the contemporary challenges reflect a crisis in the very idea of social science objectivity.

Social crises do not occur overnight; they typically develop only after a relatively lengthy gestation. Such has been true with respect to the present crisis of social science objectivity. Certain features of the present crisis—especially the passionate fervor of the participants—are reminiscent of the so-called Great Value Dispute, or *Werturteilsstreit,* which occurred between Max Weber and Gustav Schmoller and their respective followers in Germany at the turn of the century.[1] This dispute produced Weber's famous distinction between facts and values, one that is now standard fare in all introductory social science courses. Weber's arguments about this distinction are complicated, involving several important qualifications and nuances. In a broad sense, the basic distinction between facts and values derives from the difference between factual and normative knowledge. Factual knowledge is considered to be knowledge of what is, of the way things really are, comprising empirically observable matters, the natural causes of things, and so forth. Normative knowledge is considered to be knowledge of what should be, of ultimate purposes. It was Weber's position that the social sciences should be concerned exclusively with factual knowledge. The latter, he argued, should be left to individual choice or preference.

Until recently, the distinction between facts and values was accepted and taken for granted by most social scientists. Most believed that the relative objectivity of social science knowledge was assured by the self-correcting control procedures institutionalized in the traditional conception of scientific conduct known as scientific method. By establishing procedural controls for scientific observations, scientific method seeks to assure that such observations are not to any significant degree affected by the personal or subjective characteristics of the observer— such as his political, occupational, religious, ethical, or other values.

Recent intellectual developments from within many disciplines cast doubt on the validity of the traditional Weberian distinction, as well as on the promises and efficacy of the scientific method of knowing. The basic assumptions of traditional scientific method, its "metaphysics," cannot be disproven in any absolute sense. But increasingly more and more of our thoughtful social scientists are finding the traditional notions implausible. The contemporary criticism has taken several forms. Some argue that the social theories generated by the traditional methodology are not factually correct. Others say that the traditional methodology does not validly reflect actual scientific conduct. Still others claim that the traditional methodology does not have even a plausible possibility of generating valid knowledge of human activities. It is difficult to think of any criticism which could challenge the traditional goals and ideals in a more fundamental manner.

Times of intellectual crisis and passion often produce their own excesses. Such has been true of the present crisis of social science objectivity. Criticism of traditional scientific ideals has led some scholars to advocate an abandonment of concern with methods; others take contemporary critiques as an occasion for promoting a form of "antimethod." [2] Some interpret the intellectual developments and existential events of our time to mean that it is no longer meaningful to pursue the traditional goal of objective understanding; they say that all social science knowledge is necessarily subjective. From this viewpoint, the only honest scientific approach is one that is subjective.[3] But these are the extreme responses to the contemporary crisis in objectivity. Many of those who have been critical of the traditional intellectual goals and methods of the social sciences have also proposed more moderate alternatives. Both the criticism and the proposed alternatives have been varied; in one way or another, however, all reflect an interest in developing a more truthful social understanding of our daily lives.

Emerging out of all the theoretical, methodological, and philosophical debates about the social sciences is a distinct revival of interest in participant observation and field research in sociology. Field research has always been associated with a certain gaminess and adventurous zest; to a limited extent, its return to prominence is probably associated with a resurgence of these qualities in contemporary scientific practice. But the revival is also related to the abstract intellectual debates in a very fundamental way, for participant observation and field research have a direct relevance to the recent challenges to traditional conceptions of social science objectivity. To understand the nature of the crisis in objectivity and the relevance of participant observation research, it is essential to know more about the logic and rationale of traditional notions of science.

THE STANDARD VIEW OF SCIENCE:
POSITIVIST OBJECTIVISM

The intellectual foundations on which the edifice of modern science rests are conventionally termed "positivism." This term has been used during the last century to convey several distinct meanings, two of which are important here. First, positivism is generally understood to refer to a complicated philosophy of science which focuses attention on the factual character of real-world observations, thus distinguishing it from theologies and speculative philosophies. In addition, the term is also understood to refer to a very rigorous methodological program, consisting of a set of formally rational cognitive procedures usually denoted by the phrase "the scientific method." These procedures intend to screen out all effects an observer might have on propositions accorded the status of knowledge. They include specifying one's research hypotheses prior to the research and explicitly articulating one's operational definitions and measurement indices, and the evidentiary criteria that will constitute empirical support for the hypotheses.

Many of the early ideas of positivism originated in the first part of the nineteenth century. Encouraged by developments in the natural and physical sciences, the early positivists expressed an optimistic faith in the possibilities of applying the rigorous techniques of the scientific method to social phenomena. Many expressed the hope that this would generate a body of knowledge that could be used to solve man's moral, political, and other practical problems.

Positivism emerged in a context of profound changes in the societies of the West. These changes were economic, technological, political, and social in nature. They produced great dislocations and much human suffering. During this time of important social changes, increasing numbers of individuals judged the existing bodies of knowledge as inadequate to explain these events. The early beginnings of positivism in part reflected a reaction to the moral absolutism and theological dogmatism of the traditional order, which claimed absolute knowledge of reality on the basis of divine revelation and traditional dogma. The early positivists rejected these ideas about the supernaturalist–metaphysical laws of God in favor of a programmatic search for the truths of the natural world, the laws of nature. Positivism involved a methodological insistence on independent and controlled observations of naturally occurring real-world events as a condition for accepting or rejecting claims of truth. Put differently, the early positivists judged the existing bodies of knowledge to have an unexamined or "common-sense" character. They sought to formulate an alternative program to eliminate such common-sense features in favor of a scientific knowledge of reality. Distinctions between scientific and common-sense knowledge have remained with us ever since; most introductory social science classes begin with this topic.

In the late eighteenth and early nineteenth centuries, proposals to investigate the phenomena of human existence with the rigorous methods of the natural sciences were viewed by many as outrageously radical. Many felt threatened by these ideas. Such is clearly no longer the case. Most of the members of our society learn the general ideas of the scientific method at the age of eight or nine. According to the recent analyses of Israel Scheffler, a scholar favorably disposed to the traditional goals and ideals of positivist objectivism, these once-radical ideas have now achieved the status of "the standard view of science." Furthermore, this view is, in his words, "largely shared by reflective scientists, technical philosophers, and the educated public alike, and [lays] great emphasis upon the objective features of scientific thought." [4] Scheffler goes on to delineate the features of this perspective:

> We shall begin by elaborating what has above been described as the "standard view of science." Fundamentally, as we have seen, this view affirms the objectivity of science; more specifically, it understands science to be a systematic public enterprise, controlled by logic and by empirical fact, whose purpose it is to

formulate the truth about the natural world. The truth primarily sought is general, expressed in laws of nature, which tells us what is always and everywhere the case. Observation, however, supplies the particular empirical facts, the hard phenomenal data which our lawlike hypotheses strive to encompass, and for which it is the ultimate purpose of such hypotheses to account.[5]

Scheffler views positivist objectivism as promising an absolute or presuppositionless body of knowledge. The objectivity of this approach is conceived of as absolute in two distinct senses. First, the approach presupposes the existence of a social world of objective social meanings. The argument here is that the objects studied by the social sciences are essentially equivalent to the objects studied by the natural and physical sciences. The objects of this social world are considered eternal, external to the mind or consciousness of individuals, and unproblematically observed and known about in everyday life. And the social world is assumed to be so lawlike in its nature that we may reasonably hope to learn "what is always and everywhere the case." Second, and more importantly, the objectivity of this approach is considered absolute in that the technical methodological controls are considered to completely eliminate, either actually or potentially, all observer effects on the observations. The result is that the factual realities arrived at through research observations are not dependent on the knowing subject for their intelligibility. Such observations are considered objective in that they may be independently confirmed or disconfirmed by other knowing subjects at other places or times. The promise of positivist objectivism, then, is to eventually produce a body of factual knowledge about the natural world which is not dependent on the properties of any particular knowing mind or on the existential situation of that knowing mind in the world.

The major ideas of positivist objectivism have not remained static; there have been many changes and modifications during the last century. Scientific positivism is unquestionably one of the most complicated systems of social thought ever created, and hundreds of volumes are devoted to its theoretical and methodological specifics. The intention of this discussion is merely to highlight the major ideas of the hypothetical–deductive logic and methodological rationale of positivist objectivism. The methodological specifics of this scientific approach are so complicated that one contemporary scholar asserts that they are relaxed on each and every occasion of a particular research investigation. This scholar argues, furthermore, that such relaxation is inescapable.[6] Nevertheless, the abstract philosophical and theoretical ideas of positivism provided several different sets of rational cognitive criteria which were used by scientists for many years to assess the intelligibility of their efforts. It is important to understand the basic ideas of this model in order to understand the contemporary challenges to it.

THE NATURE OF THE CONTEMPORARY CRISIS IN OBJECTIVITY

Within the relatively short historical period of several hundred years, science has become a pervasive and powerful force in our contemporary world. Whatever its validity, the claim that scientific observations are objective, disinterested, and value-neutral has been important to the institutional success of science. So too has been the belief that the scientific method of knowing contains self-correcting mechanisms through which we will be led to an evolutionary progress in our understandings. During the last two decades, however, the claims made for science have been challenged on several grounds. The validity of the theories generated by the traditional methods has been questioned. The challenge has been posed of whether the traditional conceptions of scientific conduct reflect a valid account of how science is actually done. Finally, the question has been raised of whether it is theoretically and methodologically possible to study human actions with methods inherited from the natural and physical sciences.

Challenges to the validity of social theories have been the

province of the field known as sociology of knowledge—comprising metatheoretical efforts to explore the social circumstances underlying particular bodies of theoretical knowledge. In general, such theories argue that the formulation by scientists of problems, methodological procedures, grounds for inference, and criteria of validity presuppose historically relative values, ideologies, and interests. The scholarly investigations of Karl Mannheim are usually cited as landmark studies in the sociology of knowledge.[7] This intellectual field owes its good fortune of late to the insight that knowledge is a social enterprise.

C. Wright Mills's analysis of the professional ideology of social pathology is one of the best known attempts to use the insights of the sociology of knowledge to assess the validity of social theories.[8] Mills argued that the sociological conceptions employed by social pathologists were related to the shared moral perspective of their small-town, religious backgrounds. His analysis implicitly challenged social pathologists' claims of making "disinterested" scientific observations. More recently, Alvin Gouldner has analyzed the historical circumstances within which the Weberian distinction between facts and values was produced. He argues that the distinction was intended as an effort to "keep the peace" in the particular context of the German university situation at that time. While the distinction might have made some sense then, Gouldner argues that its continued use in the present American situation serves as a convenient myth.[9] The recent scholarship of Jack Douglas seeks to illuminate the strange phenomenon of why Emile Durkheim's *Suicide* was taken by many as a model for sociological inquiries.[10] Douglas argues that other's use of Durkheim's social rate approach for the study of moral phenomena is based on the ancient belief that statistical numerology is more scientific. In addition to these studies, there is a small but increasing body of evidence which documents instances when the mystique of science has been invoked to mask very narrow political interests.[11] These researches represent some of the reasons why Alvin Gouldner argues, in his controversial book *The Coming Crisis of Western Sociology,* that there exists a highly complicated "ideological substratum" for all sociological theories and methods.[12]

One argument, emanating from the Marxist scholarly tradition, asserts that any and all attempts by a given scientific investigator to render a factually correct account of an existing state of affairs represent little more than a de facto defense or justification of that state of affairs. In other words, whereas a given observer might be motivated by good intentions to render an impartial, value-free, authentic description of some aspect of society, the actual consequences of such efforts are in every case to support the established order and its ideological rationalizations. According to this argument, all claims of knowledge involve explicit and implicit political meanings. No amount of methodological rigor or observational control can make it otherwise (i.e., allegedly because of the social class structure of all capitalistic societies). Marvin Surkin argues:

> In the face of this technological explosion and increasing institutionalization and professionalization of knowledge, to claim a neutral or "objective" role for social science is clearly to fall under the onus of what Merleau-Ponty called "non-sense." Briefly put, the full thrust of reason and knowledge is being turned against itself—against truth and humanity, in favor of the dominant institutions and power-centers which are now tending to the *manipulation* rather than the *liberation* of mankind, especially its underclasses. In short, the Persuasive Neutralist who inveighs against the ideologies and utopias that want to change the world in favor of a scientific or "objective" description or interpretation of social reality turns objective knowledge upside down: a fundamentally apolitical posture becomes highly political or ideological insofar as that knowledge serves entrenched institutions and power interests, whether these be pacification programs in South Vietnam or funneling of the energies of black youth into the established channels of American society. To put it another way, the meaning and social significance of rational inquiry is inverted—sense is turned into nonsense.[13]

Surkin and many others in the social sciences who advance arguments such as the one above tend to be highly suspicious of any and all formulations of the social sciences as "quests for understanding." In Surkin's words, such a conception reflects little more than sophisticated rhetoric used to mask the real purpose of "keeping the people down." [14] According to Alvin Gouldner's recent analysis of the ideological infrastructures of scientific practice, the scientific ideal of objectivity "is the ideology of those who are alienated and politically homeless." [15] It is difficult to imagine a more unequivocal condemnation. As an alternative to the traditional interpretation of science as a quest for understanding, those making this argument propose a conception of social science as political action either maintaining, or intending the transformation of, the existing order.

Criticism of social science knowledge on the basis of its tacit political meanings, functions, consequences, or uses is at least partially justified. This is recognized by many who are otherwise known for their traditional or conservative views. Social theorist Robert Nisbet, for example, states that he views the recent attacks on the objectivity of the social sciences as "the most unbelievable thing" of the contemporary scene in the American universities.[16] Having expressed his personal feelings of chagrin, Nisbet goes on to acknowledge the lamentable relationship between the social sciences and the official agencies of social control which have developed in the United States since the end of the Second World War.

The argument that all claims of scientific knowledge reflect tacit political meanings is in one sense, however, a tautology. If all claims of knowledge reflect the social and political context in which they are produced, then how does one escape from this trap to gain a realization that this is indeed what is going on? Some of the critical and radical social scientists have recognized this dilemma. Several of the most severe critics of contemporary social science admit that the enterprise possesses *both* conservative and liberating potentials. It is not a dilemma which is easily resolved. In Gouldner's recent work, for example, he advances what, as we have seen, has to be the most unequivocal condemnation of social science objectivity. In proposing his alternative vision of a reflexive sociology, however, Gouldner reaffirms several features of the traditional objectivity ideals.[17]

Inquiries in the sociology of knowledge generally argue that a given body of putative scientific knowledge is related to one or more conditions left unexamined in the original research. Such conditions may include societal or existential circumstances, class interests, personal values, and so forth. Defenders of the traditional goals and methods of science say that while such findings might be plausibly interpreted as limitations of science as it now exists, they do not necessarily falsify the hypothetical–deductive *logic* of scientific methodology. Israel Scheffler, for example, is one of those who argues that there is no *logical* inconsistency between sociology of knowledge findings and the traditional methods of science; there is no reason why such findings cannot be stated in propositional form, measured, and made public for the independent verification of others.[18] Findings from the sociology of knowledge may point out many limitations of the traditional goals and methods of science, but they do not, in and of themselves, constitute a challenge to the foundations of traditional science.

Another challenge stems from the contemporary researches of several physiological, cognitive, and social psychologists. These researches show that what a given individual perceives, or regards as a fact, is highly variable. For example, experiments in physiological psychology conducted by McClelland and Atkinson led them to argue that what an individual "sees" is to some extent relative to his physical condition at the time of observation.[19] Researches by cognitive and social psychologists indicate that one's state of expectation, frame of reference, mental set, or conceptual schema will influence what one "sees." [20] And a vast body of materials from the field of linguistics, especially those following in the vein of Sapir and Whorf, lead many to argue that language is not simply a medium for reporting what one observes, but rather plays a crucial role in *defining* what it is one observes.[21] For the present discussion, the major point of these researches is that what was at one time conceived of by the practitioners of positivist objectivism as a relatively unproblematic "factual observation" is now viewed by more and more thoughtful scholars as much more complicated, variable, and contingent. These findings imply that a scientific investigator is not a passive receptacle for empirical observations, but rather actively contributes to what is observed and reported as fact. Because of this, then, these researches are properly seen as constituting a more serious challenge to traditional scientific method than the findings of the sociology of knowledge.

Scholars from several disciplines, then, contend that the abstract methodological program of positivist objectivism does not accurately describe how scientific conduct is actually done. Recent analyses by historians and philosophers of science constitute one of the major challenges to what Scheffler has called the standard view of science. The most provocative argument put forth in recent years is that of Thomas Kuhn in *The Structure of Scientific Revolutions.*[22] This scholarly work has stimulated much controversy.[23] Kuhn's analysis involves a theoretical interpretation of a vast range of historical materials drawn from most of the sciences. He challenges the belief that the rigorous observational controls of the traditional methodology are of a self-correcting nature that they progressively eliminate biases and errors. According to Kuhn, disciplined commitment to these ideals of methodology has not in fact been shown to purge claims of truth of any and all common-sense elements.

Kuhn argues that everyday scientific practice occurs within the boundaries of a given "paradigm," or model. The model specifies what are to be considered the appropriate problems for investigation, the relevant facts for the purposes of the inquiry, appropriate methods of inquiry, criteria for drawing inferences from factual realities to more general, abstract, or theoretical statements, and so on. Kuhn says that the model might even include a generally accepted notion about the "anomalies" or "contradictions" within the model itself, that is, phenomena recognized to fall outside of what the model can explain, but for which there exists a hope that an explanation might be forthcoming with additional research. Kuhn then argues, when viewed historically, scientific progress has not proven to result from the progressive elimination of biases through methodological controls, but rather the creative advances in science typically originate from *outside* the boundaries of the "normal paradigm" of scientific conduct—that is, from different models, theories, or conceptions of facts. Kuhn's argument directly challenges the taken-for-granted belief in the evolutionary progress of scientific knowledge. He says that the history of scientific advance is more truthfully one of breakthroughs, or what he calls "scientific revolutions."

Kuhn's analysis about the nature of everyday scientific work appears to correspond to the reflections of the famous physicist Max Planck. Planck wrote in his autobiography, "A new scientific truth does not triumph by convincing its opponents and making them see the light, but rather because its opponents eventually die, and a new generation grows up that is familiar with it." [24] Understanding the relevance of Kuhn's thesis to the previous discussions of the positivist objectivist model is facilitated by the following analogy. Just as con men, prostitutes, heroin users, ghetto residents, politicians, and used-car salesmen have their own distinctive argot and body of common-sense knowledge with which to make sense out of their respective life situations, so do various groups of scientists have their peculiar criteria of knowledge which they find subjectively meaningful as a way of making sense out of their respective realities. As with religious symbols and myths, each such scientific symbology may be experienced by its users as subjectively and existentially "real." [25] But the factual relationships between such cognitive criteria and empirical reality rest on the common-sense presuppositions of particular collectivities of scientists.

Kuhn's contentions about the nature of daily scientific conduct are formulated at a relatively high level of abstraction.

Other scholars have challenged Kuhn's assertions with charges of conceptual ambiguity or have arrived at different interpretations of the historical materials. But there is a considerable body of empirical evidence from other sources which tends to support Kuhn's analysis. This evidence comes from those who have studied traditional research as it is actually done in scientific work. One important source of evidence is the retrospective reflections of practicing scientists, but there are empirical studies as well. The researches of Harold Garfinkel, for example, led him to argue that the canons of objectivity which require a literal description of the phenomenon of inquiry are relaxed on each and every occasion of an actual investigation.[26] In the same vein, Aaron Cicourel argues that the numerical and mathematical properties presupposed by what is conventionally understood as "hard data" in sociology do not meet the requirements for literal measurement of social actions.[27] Since the numerical data used in many sociological researches fails to meet the formal properties of reflexivity, symmetry, and transitivity which are necessary if they are to be treated as real numbers, the question is raised of how they are actually used by scientists. Cicourel says that these numerical data are typically employed in a metaphorical or synecdochical fashion. This represents, according to his analysis, "measurement by fiat," and how the social actions observed are interpreted to achieve these numerical representations remains an open question.

The research experiences of Jack Douglas led him to make still another argument. On the basis of his studies of suicidal phenomena and the uses of official statistics on suicide, Douglas says that traditional researchers relax the canons of literal measurement in order to sneak in, or "bootleg," their subjective, common-sense understandings of suicide.[28] Similar documentation is given to us by Rosalie Wax. Reflecting at considerable length on her research career, she indicates that such phenomena are not restricted to statistical analyses. During her field research at the Japanese relocation centers during World War II, Wax observes, she instructed the research subjects as to the in formation she wanted to find out from them.[29] Herbert Gans's reflections on his field researches challenge even the unwritten rule that a scientist should be honest. Gans argues that a researcher necessarily has to be dishonest in order to collect "honest data." [30]

The researches and arguments mentioned here represent only a small portion of the empirical evidence which tends to support Thomas Kuhn's analysis of the nature of everyday scientific conduct. Our discussion has been only cursory in nature, but it is sufficient to indicate that the current crisis of social science objectivity runs deeper than the long-standing disputes about the relative differences between hard and soft data, quantitative and qualitative methods, and so on.

At a more abstract level, challenges to the objectivity of existing social science knowledge involve issues of epistemology, or theories of knowledge. On some occasions the epistemological arguments are combined with some of those noted briefly above; [31] on other occasions scholars distinguish between the epistemological and political arguments.[32] These arguments generally focus on one of two different types of problems. The first involves the argument that the objects of social science knowledge—human activities—involve certain distinctive features which are fundamentally different from the objects studied by the natural and physical sciences. Accordingly, goes this argument, the social sciences require the adoption of a distinctive methodology which remains true to the distinctive subject matter. The second argument contends that the social science methodologies modeled after those of the natural sciences are themselves nonobjective because they are not founded on cognitive criteria shared by the scientific observer and the subjects of the inquiry. It is clear that there is a close affinity between these two lines of argument.

At the heart of most of the scholarly inquiries of social and cultural reality that originate from the traditions of German Idealism is the conception of the distinctive subject matter of the social sciences. Those advancing this position say that the objects of social science knowledge are fundamentally different from the material and physical objects studied by the natural sciences. The point is made that the "objects" of social science investigations experience their actions as subjectively meaningful (or meaningless). Indeed, they are not "objects" at all, in the conventional sense, but acting subjects. Thus, the meaning of an action from the actor's perspective must be taken into account if one desires a true (or intersubjective) understanding. In line with this conception of social action, many scholars have argued that the hypothetical–deductive methodology of positivist objectivism presupposes the observer's omniscience in knowing the actor's meanings. This is so because the traditional model stipulates that one must hypothetically specify the meanings of the phenomena prior to making any observations; in a very real sense, the practitioners of positivist objectivism decide on a common-sense, subjective basis what will count as an empirical observation even before his research begins. As an alternative to this approach, those advancing this argument propose some form of participation with the members of the setting studied in order to gain an empathetic understanding of their actions. The proposed objective of this is to "get inside" the actor's perspective, to understand the situation from that stance, so as to work up to more general, theoretical understandings from that starting point.

The debate between those who say that the objects of study in the social sciences are essentially similar to those objects studied by the natural and physical sciences and those who argue that the subjective meaningfulness of social phenomena gives the social sciences a distinctive subject matter is a long-standing one. In traditional intellectual terms, this debate is often conceived of as the struggle between the competing theories of knowledge stemming from the traditions of British Empiricism and German Idealism. But such a distinction is also a great oversimplification of the issues. The social meaningfulness of the phenomena under investigation is a necessary assumption of *all* empirical inquiry, and not merely a question of one's philosophical "choice" or preference. The practice of social science becomes intelligible as a human enterprise only with this assumption.

It is clear, then, that more and more scholars no longer find the claims of positivist objectivism plausible. The promise of positivism was to produce an objective body of knowledge, that is, a body of knowledge independent of the properties of any particular knowing mind. But, as we have seen from a variety of perspectives, knowledge is at least to some extent dependent on the knowing subject.

To say that knowledge is dependent on the knowing subject raises the issue of solipsism. "Solipsism" is the term used to refer to a theory of knowledge which asserts that all social reality exists only as a function of the internal mental states of the self. While the theory may express a logically possible consequence of abandoning the categorical subject–object dualism of the traditional theories, the prima facie evidence against its validity is overwhelming. If, for example, the knowing act were entirely subjective in nature, then one would expect to find as many social theories as there are social theorists. As a matter of fact, however, there are thousands of theorists, but only a virtual handful of social theories.

This discussion has presented only the barest details of a small portion of the critical debates bearing on the current crisis in social science objectivity. The discussion does suffice, however, to indicate that the challenge to what Scheffler has called the standard view of scientific conduct is mounted from many directions. It is wrong to think that these challenges constitute any kind of "united front" against the traditional order. The differences among the critics themselves are at least as great as those between the critics and the traditionalists. The diverse nature of these arguments cannot be overemphasized. They are not additive. They do not constitute a "whole." Even the evaluations of their implications vary. At the most charitable level, the critiques amount to a charge of perpetuating the banal conceits of past traditions. At the least charitable, they add up to a charge of selling these banal conceits to the highest bidder. In either case, the contemporary objectivity crisis calls into question the personal integrity and authenticity of those who practice social science.

ALTERNATIVE PROPOSALS

During the last decade there have emerged several attempts to formulate creative alternatives to the no longer tenable absolutist conception of objectivity. David Matza, John Lofland, and several other symbolic interactionists in sociology, for example, propose a naturalistic perspective for a more truthful understanding of human actions.[33] Peter Berger proposes a humanistic perspective.[34] There have been several different proposals for a radical or critical perspective.[35] Increasing interest in the scholarly analyses of phenomenologists such as Edmund Husserl and Alfred Schutz has inspired proposals for a phenomenological sociology.[36] Harold Garfinkel, Aaron Cicourel, and others extend the methods of the phenomenologists to a disciplined form of research called ethnomethodology, or "neopraxiology." [37] Jack Douglas and others have promoted an existential phenomenology as an alternative program for sociology.[38] Melvin Pollner promotes a transcendental anthropology as a new motif for sociological investigations.[39] Stanford Lyman and Marvin Scott claim that their new proposals synthesize several of the above into what they call a "sociology of the absurd." [40] Two recent proposals intend a synthesis of the emerging interests in phenomenology and Marxism. Alvin Gouldner calls for the development of a reflexive sociology; [41] John O'Neill proposes a reconceptualization of the sociological enterprise as a "skin trade." [42]

All of these proposals reject the subject–object dualism underlying the traditional scientific theories and methods, recognizing instead the interdependency between the knowing subject and the objects of knowledge. David Matza's proposal of a naturalistic perspective for sociology illustrates this:

> Naturalism when applied to the study of man has no choice but to conceive man as subject precisely because naturalism claims fidelity to the empirical world. In the empirical world, man is subject and not object, except when he is likened to one by himself or by another subject. Naturalism must choose the subjective view, and consequently it must combine the scientific method with the distinctive tools of humanism—experience, intuition, and empathy. Naturalism has no other choice because its philosophical commitment is neither to objectivity nor subjectivity, neither to scientific method nor humanist sensibility. Its only commitment is fidelity to the phenomenon under consideration. Thus, in the study of man, there is no antagonism between naturalism and a repudiation of the objective view, nor a contradiction between naturalism and the humane methods of experience, reason, intuition, and empathy. Naturalism in the study of man is a disciplined humanism.[43]

Matza's naturalistic perspective, in common with the other proposed alternatives, is based on the perception that the cultural realities which sociology seeks to understand are inherently without objective meaning. These realities consist of the societal members' subjectively meaningful interpretations of their experiences and life situations. So it is the actors' interpretations which must be taken into account if one is to have knowledge which is "objective" (i.e., based on intersubjectively shared criteria). Thus, as an alternative to the objectivity of positivist objectivism, Matza envisions a body of knowledge which maintains "the fidelity of the phenomenon under consideration." Similar ideas are found in the other alternative proposals as well, expressed in such phrases as "maintaining the integrity of the phenomenon," "being faithful to the existential experiences of the subjects," "remaining true to the actor's perspective," "viewing the subjects of sociological inquiries as brother sociologists," and so on.

There is still some question as to whether these newly articulated faiths can take the place of the complicated ideas of the positivist models. As mentioned earlier in this chapter, practitioners of positivism developed a complex normative solution to the problem of objectivity, involving formally rational observational controls. This model provided a set of criteria against which the validity or reliability of a given study could be assessed. Even when the criteria of this model were relaxed in all specific applications, the model provided ways of "making sense" of the efforts. How many times have all of us heard a research derided, for example, for "having a small N" (or number of observations)? Matza's alternative, along with the others, essentially proposes an interpretive solution to the problem of objectivity. It is an "interpretive solution" in that we are asked to locate the foundations of a truthful knowledge of our cultural realities in our everyday, common-sense experiences as societal members, including our self-reflexive understandings of those experiences. This reflects a recognition that objectivity, or intersubjectivity, is not a matter of abiding by the formally rational rules of a model; rather, it involves a substantively rational relationship between the knowing subject and one's fellow human actors.

IMPLICATIONS OF THE PROBLEMS IN OBJECTIVITY FOR FIELD RESEARCH

What do these abstract arguments about the relationship between knowledge and the properties of the human knowing mind have to do with participant observation and field research in sociology? The full ramifications are unclear in any absolute sense, at least at this time. But these abstract philosophical considerations do imply a fundamental reconceptualization of participant observation research. They suggest that, in the most basic sense, all social science knowledge is grounded in our everyday lives. Furthermore, all of our observations of the empirical realities in our daily lives are rendered socially intelligible and meaningful only by and through our participation as societal members. This membership brings with it a vast reservoir of "common-sense" knowledge, role conceptions, typifications, and so on. And our acquisition of such "cultural knowledge" precedes our learning of scientific theory and method. In the most basic sense, then, all empirical investigations in the social sciences involve participant observation in that they necessarily presuppose these social competencies. This is true of laboratory or experimental research, surveys and interviews, and field research. Field research is distinguished from the others in that it tries to ground its empirical observations in the intersubjective cognitive criteria actually used by societal members in their daily life situations. If this were all there was to it, however, field research would be indistinguishable from other forms of common-sense inquiry, such as journalism or detective work. The major point is that the observation of naturally occurring everyday events yields the fundamental data for building a more abstract (or theoretical) understanding of the basic properties of human existence.

That field research tries to ground empirical observations in the intersubjective criteria should not be taken to imply that it is the only legitimate form of scientific inquiry. If one wanted to study nonmeaningful behaviors such as the basic physiological properties of the human body, for example, then it is clear that field research would be very inappropriate for this; rather, laboratory or experimental research would be the best approach. If one wanted to study social actions which were not morally meaningful to the members of society, such as how much milk individuals consume every day, then it would seem that questionnaire or survey research would be a much better approach than field research. What form of participant observational research is elected for a particular study, then, will be partially related to the nature of the research problem at hand and the type of information sought.

Although all field researches are guided by the intention to transcend the subjective observational categories of the researcher—to base the observations in intersubjective categories, at least insofar as this is possible—there are different varieties of field research. One type is *substantive* field research. The purpose of a substantive field investigation is to produce a theoretical understanding of the substantive social realities of a particular setting. In the social welfare offices I studied, for example, the primary substantive realities were working with people, or "people work," and paperwork. But these were not the only realities of the setting; there were many others which I did not investigate, such as the social workers' recreational activities, their love affairs and family lives, and so forth. A substantive field research project seeks to give the reader a sense of "the action" taking place in a particular setting; as such, it strives for a certain measure of representativeness in the observations.

Another type of field research is *basic theoretical* field research. This type of inquiry has little interest in substantive realities. It is guided by the purpose of analyzing the essential or fundamental properties of human communication or interpretation. A field researcher interested in basic theory might study a factory, for example, but the research report would tell us little about what goes on inside the factory. Instead, it might tell us about the essential properties of talking, which the factory workers take for granted in their daily routines.

Hence, even though all field researchers try to understand the meanings of the actions they observe to those in the setting, the observational data still do not "speak for themselves." What gets observed as well as how the data are organized into an analysis are still dependent on the observer's perspective and purposes.

Matza's book *Becoming Deviant* illustrates these ambiguities.[44] After an insightful review of previous theories and researches in the field of deviant behavior, Matza depicts the process of becoming a deviant as involving one of three "master conceptions." He terms these master conceptions affinity, affiliation, and signification. His argument is that these three master conceptions represent "strategies of explanation" for understanding how an individual becomes a deviant. But the reader is not told about the bases on which these conceptions are developed. Do they reflect the types of explanations given by the individuals themselves as to why or how they became deviant? Or do they represent the author's creative formulations? These questions remain unanswered.

At the most basic level, the contemporary objectivity crisis stems from the personal involvement of the observer in the very settings he seeks to observe, record, and understand. Sociologists of knowledge claim that all researches presuppose historically relative values and interests. Defenders of the traditional ideals respond to this argument by saying that scientists should make their personal values explicit.[45] The scholarly writings of philosophers and historians of science indicate, however, that the observer's personal values, while not completely irrelevant, tend to be relatively unimportant in the organization of the factual realities of a research investigation. What appears to be more basic than the observer's values are the concomitants of membership in a scientific community. In substantive terms, these include feelings of loyalty and comradeship as well as emotional commitments to theories or methodologies. The danger here is that an investigator may interpret the observational realities in the setting in terms which are subjectively meaningful to the members of his scientific subculture. There is a small but growing body of literature which suggests this possibility with respect to previous social science researches. Almost a decade after the publication of his award-winning *Delinquency and Drift,* for example, David Matza informed us that the entire research was related to his political commitments at the time.[46] One could not detect this from reading the book, however. Several decades after her researches in the Japanese relocation centers, Rosalie Wax tells us that she instructed her intimates about what she wanted to find out from them.[47] Again, this was not apparent from reading the research report. There are many other examples of this as well.[48] The practice of field research, then, clearly does not guarantee the objectivity of a research report. Unless further elaborated, the proposed alternatives to the objectivity of positivist objectivism would appear to have no immediately obvious advantages over the traditional ideas.

That social scientists are part of the phenomena they seek to understand is the irremediable paradox of our search for a truthful self-understanding. The observer's embeddedness in the observations raises two important questions. The first is whether the observer's participation with the members of a social setting introduces any greater bias or error than would otherwise obtain from a sole reliance on one's uncorrected presumptions about the meanings of social actions. Previous discussions in this chapter indicate that the evidence bearing on this issue is mixed. On the one hand, one might think that experimental research would introduce the least observer influence because of the laboratory controls over the observations. But there is convincing evidence that this is not necessarily true. Experimental researches are situationally bounded. An experimenter's interpretations of the meanings of actions in the laboratory may bear little relation to the meaning of those events as they occur naturally in daily life. While seemingly involving the least potential for the observer's "contamination" by the subjects, then, experimental research may be very biased indeed. The previous discussions also show, on the other hand, that participating with the members during a field research project does not automatically produce intersubjective results. It is still possible that a field researcher could interpret the observational realities in terms that are meaningful only to the members of his scientific subculture. Adopting one form of participant observation over another, then, does not guarantee objectivity.

The second major question is the inevitable tension between empathy and sympathy. Field research has long been considered justified because it affords an empathetic understanding of the meanings of events to those in a given setting. An empathic understanding results when the observer is able to understand daily events as the members experience them. To achieve this, the observer goes through a learning process which is similar to that of a neophyte member. If others develop feelings of trust toward the observer to the extent of sharing their private thoughts, feelings, and perceptions, close personal ties will undoubtedly result. The development of such ties raises the possibility that the observer will adopt a sympathetic stance toward the objects of his research. A sympathetic stance is one wherein the observer takes the side of the group which is studied, and hence feels bound to demonstrate the validity and correctness of that perspective. Adopting a sympathetic stance toward the subjects of one's observations is so common that some scholars recommend that we should always read field reports with an understanding of the tenuous nature of the distinction between sympathy and empathy.[49]

In the remaining chapters, I present a detailed account of my field research experiences in social welfare offices. The original plans for the research called for an analysis of the nature of social casework practice. These plans changed during the research, which eventually resulted in two separate research reports.[50] The following chapters reflect the decision to pay attention to the research process while investigating the daily realities of public welfare. Conscious efforts were directed toward recording field notes of the research experience and the social workers' perceptions of it.

These experiences have led me to draw several conclusions about the conduct of sociological field research. First, the accounts found in the traditional literature tend to be highly overformalized and overrationalized. They conspicuously fail to capture the emergent and problematic nature of actual research conduct. Second, the problems of producing an objective research report are not readily solved by the self-conscious decision to "maintain the integrity of the phenomenon under consideration," or to adopt an empathetic rather than a sympathetic stance toward the subjects of ones observations. Third, because certain features of any research project are beyond the control of the field researcher, it is incumbent on the researcher to use his or her sociological competencies to evaluate the effects of these features on the observations. These points will be discussed in greater detail in the chapters that follow.

NOTES

1. See Ralf Dahrendorf, "Values and Social Sciences: The Value Dispute in Perspective," pp. 1–18 in his *Essays in the Theory of Society*. Stanford: Stanford University Press, 1968.

2. See, for example, Derek L. Phillips, *Abandoning Method*. San Francisco: Jossey-Bass, 1973. Also, Charles Hampden-Turner, *Radical Man*. Garden City, N.Y.: Doubleday-Anchor, 1971.

3. See Marvin Surkin, "Sense and Non-Sense in Politics." In Alan Wolfe and Marvin Surkin, eds., *An End to Political Science*. New York: Basic Books, 1970.

4. Israel Scheffler, *Science and Subjectivity*. Indianapolis: Bobbs-Merrill, 1967, p. 7.

5. *Ibid.*, p. 8.

6. Harold Garfinkel, *Studies in Ethnomethodology*. Englewood Cliffs, N.J.: Prentice-Hall, 1967, p. 6.

7. Karl Mannheim, *Ideology & Utopia*. Translated by Louis Wirth and Edward Shils. New York: Harcourt, Brace & World, 1936.

8. C. Wright Mills, "The Professional Ideology of Social Pathologists," *American Journal of Sociology,* 49 (September 1942): 165–80.

9. Alvin W. Gouldner, "Anti-Minotaur: The Myth of a Value-Free Sociology," *Social Problems,* 9 (Winter 1962): 199–213.

10. Jack D. Douglas, "The Rhetoric of Science and the Origins of Statistical Social Thought," pp. 44–57 in Edward A. Tiryakian, ed., *The Phenomenon of Sociology*. New York: Appleton-Century-Crofts, 1971.

11. The best illustration of this is the infamous "Project Camelot." See Irving Louis Horowitz, "The Life and Death of Project Cam-

elot," *Trans-action*, 3 (November–December, 1970): 3–7. See also Ralph L. Beals, *Politics of Social Research*. Chicago: Aldine, 1969.

12. Alvin W. Gouldner, *The Coming Crisis of Western Sociology*. New York: Basic Books, 1970.

13. Marvin Surkin, *op. cit.*, pp. 25–26.

14. *Ibid.*, p. 27.

15. Alvin W. Gouldner, *op. cit.*

16. Robert Nisbet, "Subjective Si! Objective No!," *The New York Review of Books*, April 5, 1970, pp. 1–2, 36–37.

17. Alvin W. Gouldner, *op. cit.*, esp. pp. 481–512.

18. See, Israel Scheffler, *op. cit.*

19. D. C. McClelland and J. W. Atkinson, "The Projective Expression of Needs: I, The Effect of Differential Intensities of the Hunger Drive on Perception," *Journal of Psychology*, 25, (1948): 205–22.

20. References are made to the following researches: Jerome S. Bruner, Jacqueline J. Goodnow, George A. Austin, *A Study of Thinking*. New York: John Wiley, 1956. Muzafer Sherif and Hadley Cantril, *The Psychology of Ego Involvements*. New York: John Wiley, 1947; Martin Scheerer, "Cognitive Theory." In Gardner Lindzey, ed., *Handbook of Social Psychology*. Reading, Mass.: Addison-Wesley, 1954.

21. B. J. Whorf, *Language, Thought, and Reality*. New York: John Wiley, 1956. The implications of the Sapir–Whorf hypothesis for the conduct of empirical sociological researches are discussed in Aaron V. Cicourel, *Method and Measurement in Sociology*. New York: The Free Press, 1964.

22. Chicago: The University of Chicago Press, 1962. Revised Edition, 1970.

23. See Imre Lakatos and Alan Musgrave, eds., *Criticism and the Growth of Knowledge*. New York: Cambridge University Press, 1970.

24. Max Planck, *Scientific Autobiography and Other Papers*. Translated by Frank Gaynor. New York: Philosophical Library, 1949, pp. 33–34.

25. Robert Bellah makes this point in reference to religious symbols. See his "Christianity and Symbolic Realism," *Journal for the Scientific Study of Religion,* 9 (Summer, 1970): 77–92.

26. Harold Garfinkel, *op. cit.*

27. Aaron Cicourel, *op. cit.* Cicourel expresses his indebtedness to Garfinkel for suggesting the usage of metaphor and synecdoch in this context.

28. Jack Douglas, *op. cit.* See also his *The Social Meanings of Suicide.* Princeton, N.J.: Princeton University Press, 1967; and "Understanding Everyday Life," pp. 3–44 in Jack D. Douglas, ed., *Understanding Everyday Life.* Chicago: Aldine, 1970.

29. Rosalie H. Wax, *Doing Fieldwork.* Chicago: The University of Chicago Press, 1972, p. 76.

30. Herbert Gans, "The Participant Observer as a Human Being," pp. 300–17 in Howard S. Becker, Blanche Geer, David Riesman, and Robert S. Weiss, eds., *Institutions and the Person.* Chicago: Aldine, 1968.

31. See Marvin Surkin, *loc. cit.*

32. See Abraham Kaplan, *The Conduct of Inquiry.* San Francisco: Chandler, 1964, esp. pp. 370–87.

33. See John F. Lofland, "Notes on Naturalism in Sociology," *Kansas Journal of Sociology,* III, 2 (Spring, 1967): 45–61; David Matza, *Becoming Deviant.* Englewood Cliffs, N.J.: Prentice-Hall, 1969; Barney G. Glaser and Anselm Strauss, *The Discovery of Grounded Theory.* Chicago: Aldine, 1967.

34. See Peter L. Berger, *Invitation to Sociology: A Humanistic Perspective.* Garden City, N.Y.: Doubleday, 1963; Severyn T. Bruyn, *The Humanistic Perspective in Sociology.* Englewood Cliffs, N.J.: Prentice-Hall, 1966.

35. As an example, see the essays in George Fischer, ed., *The Revival of American Socialism: Selected Papers of the Socialist Scholar's Conference.* New York: Oxford University Press, 1971.

36. See, for example, George Psathas, ed., *Phenomenological Sociology.* New York: John Wiley, forthcoming.

37. Harold Garfinkel, *op. cit.;* Aaron Cicourel, *op. cit.*

38. See Jack D. Douglas, ed., *Existential Sociology,* forthcoming.

39. Melvin Pollner, "On the Foundations of Mundane Reasoning," unpublished PhD dissertation, Department of Sociology, University of California, Santa Barbara, 1970.

40. Stanford M. Lyman and Marvin B. Scott, *A Sociology of the Absurd*. New York: Appleton-Century-Crofts, 1970.

41. Alvin W. Gouldner, *op. cit.*

42. John O'Neill, "Sociology as a Skin Trade," *Sociological Inquiry*, 40 (Winter, 1971): 76–91.

43. David Matza, *op. cit.*, p. 8.

44. *Ibid.*

45. Gunnar Myrdal, *Objectivity in Social Research*. New York: Pantheon, 1969.

46. The reference here is taken from Joseph G. Weis, "Dialogue with David Matza," *Issues in Criminology*, 6, 1 (Winter, 1971): 35–53.

47. See Rosalie Wax, *loc. cit.*

48. The most famous (or infamous) example would be the debates between Oscar Lewis and Robert Redfield about their respective researches in Tepoztlan. The reader is also referred to the essays collected in Irving L. Horowitz, ed., *Sociological Self-Images*. Beverly Hills, Calif.: Sage, 1969.

49. W. Richard Scott, "Field Methods in the Study of Organizations," pp. 272–82 in James G. March, ed., *Handbook of Organizations*. Chicago: Rand-McNally, 1962.

50. John M. Johnson, "The Social Construction of Official Information," unpublished PhD dissertation, University of California, San Diego, 1973; also, *Doing Social Casework*, unpublished manuscript.

Chapter 2

The Research Settings
and Their Contexts

THE PURPOSE of this chapter is to provide the reader with background information on the origins, development, and contemporary status of public welfare programs and on the Child Welfare Services (CWS) settings wherein my research investigations were conducted. My intention is not to provide a history either of public assistance programs or of the development of the social work profession; [1] rather, the purpose here is to familiarize the reader with selected aspects of the research settings, and of the atmosphere currently surrounding social welfare practice, which are important to an understanding of our research. In addition, descriptive and documentary materials are presented to give a flavor of the daily activities that take place in these settings.

The initial plans for this research project originated in the fall of 1969. Several of the initial interviews were conducted in October, November, and December of that year. That portion of the research plan which obligated the observer to participate with the social workers in their everyday activities occurred primarily between May, 1970, and May, 1971. While the research observations eventually included a total of five district welfare offices located in two metropolitan county departments of public welfare, the observations in four of these five offices were limited to one week or less. The major portion of the research occurred at one agency, an office referred to throughout this report as the "Metro office." This research was conducted primarily between July, 1970, and May, 1971, during which the author participated in everyday work routines on a regular basis. Following these ten months at the Metro office, additional observations at several agencies were made on an irregular basis. I have continued to maintain contact with several of the members of these agencies since the actual field observations were completed.[2]

Throughout the duration of the research project (1969–72), the topics of public assistance and social work received considerable attention from all of the mass media. All three major television networks carried many news stories, and documentaries to discuss these issues. The program schedules of local radio and television stations reflected similar concerns. Many major national magazines published articles on the problems of public welfare, and each of the national news magazines carried at least one cover story on welfare during this period. The phenomena included under the general term "welfare" were commonly seen as constituting a national social problem of crisis proportions. This was evident in the language of these articles, which included such phraseology as "the welfare maze," "the shame of a nation," "time for welfare reform," "the welfare nightmare," and "welfare—the best of intentions, the worst of results." [3]

At about this same time, California Governor Ronald Reagan described the welfare programs of his state as "a three billion dollar moral and administrative disaster, a way of life without a goal, a road that can only lead to bankruptcy—in human terms it is a tragic failure." [4] Throughout this period, concerned individuals were trying to figure out why welfare rolls and expenditures were "skyrocketing." One scholarly work which addressed these issues directly was *Regulating the Poor* (1971), by Frances Fox Piven and Richard A. Cloward, which received the prestigious C. Wright Mills award in sociology. In it the authors argued that the welfare explosion of the 1960s was "designed to mute civil disorder," which according to them represented one of two cyclical trends embedded in the underlying logic of capitalist economics.[5] My own scope and purposes in undertaking this research were far more limited than those of Piven and Cloward, however. My original purpose was to describe and analyze in some detail how the members of several social settings organized their everyday affairs. Specifically, the observations focused on the activities of those social workers engaged in child welfare services. Their work constituted a relatively small proportion of the activities comprehended by the various public welfare programs. Most of the field observations were conducted in one office, where CWS social workers numbered only a little more than a dozen out of the 270 total employees.

PUBLIC WELFARE: FINANCIAL AID AND ASSISTANCE

Public welfare involves, at the least, the provision of financial aid to those judged to be in need of such assistance. Historical analyses of the concept of public welfare in the West generally trace its origins back to Biblical writings or, more commonly, to the initial English Poor Laws enacted in 1601. Those concerned with tracing the development of American social policy in the field of welfare typically point out the existence, since the early decades of the nineteenth century, of a wide range of private welfare agencies which dispensed financial aid and other aid to those considered less fortunate. One of the first private social welfare agencies in the United States was the New York Society for the Prevention of Cruelty to Children, an outgrowth of the similarly named organization seeking to prevent cruelty to animals.

The provision of financial assistance to the needy poor by public or governmental agencies in the United States occurred irregularly during the first decades of the twentieth century. For the most part it can be said that public welfare or public assistance programs as we know them today began with the passage of the Social Security Act of 1935. Intended as a remedy for some of the complex problems emerging out of the Great Depression, it was this piece of federal legislation which established the concept of federal–state–county "partnerships" for the provision of assistance of various "categories" of needy persons. The Social Security Act of 1935 has been subject to a long series of modifications and amendments throughout the years, but despite these many changes, the categorical approach remains the definitive characteristic of contemporary financial assistance programs throughout the United States. For this reason, the financial assistance provided under the auspices of the Social Security Act is commonly referred to as categorical aid.

The categories of aid included under the original act were: Old Age Security (OAS), Aid to Families with Dependent Children (AFDC), Aid to the Blind (AB), and Aid to the Totally Disabled (ATD).[6] All of these programs were voluntary rather than mandatory with respect to participation of the states, but all of the states and territories took advantage of the matching-grant provisions. Subsequent amendments to the act (in 1961 and 1962) added two more categories, Aid to Families with Dependent Children–Unemployed Parents (AFDC–U) and Boarding Homes and Institutions (BHI). (While all of the states have availed themselves of the latter, only twenty-four out of fifty-three eligible states and territories have availed themselves of the provisions of the AFDC–U program.) In addition, there are two so-called residual aid programs, comprising financial assistance completely funded by the state or county resources and not subject to federal subsidy. These are Aid to the Potentially

Self-Supporting Blind (APSB), in which the program and administrative costs are typically shared by state and local levels of government, and General Assistance (also called General Relief, or GR), which is completely funded by the local or county government. The administration of this latter program is widely recognized as fluctuating greatly in accordance with the whims and budgetary practicalities of local political expediency.

In Western State (see note 2), besides the eight primary public assistance programs there are many other welfare programs either totally or partially administered by other agencies, some directly and others indirectly related to the public welfare programs. In addition, the directories of potential resources for social casework services in Northern and Southern Metropolitan Counties include several hundred other private agencies. In view of this situation, it is not surprising that the County Welfare Directors Association of Western State began a recent report with the observation that the so-called public welfare system in their state fails to meet every one of the definitive criteria for a "system," typically defined as a set arrangement of thinking so related or connected as to form a unity or organic whole.

PUBLIC WELFARE: THE EMERGENCE OF PUBLIC SOCIAL SERVICES

Today the concept of public welfare is often equated with the provision of what are termed social services by professional social workers. But the provision by government of social services is of much more recent origin than the 1935 Social Security Act.

Giving charity to the poor has been commonplace in Western societies for centuries. During the nineteenth century, however, such activities began to take on new meanings. With the ascendancy of the middle classes, poverty came to be seen as having moral roots. This attitude eventually gave rise to that loosely allied congeries of organizations we now refer to as the "Charity Organization Movement'' which sought to subordinate the giving of alms or charity to the task of reforming the moral character of the poor.

Throughout the nineteenth century a set of scientifically based techniques was codified to serve this purpose. The technique of friendly visiting between volunteer members of charity organizations and the poor was conceived as being, in Paine's words, ''the only hope of civilization against the gathering curse of pauperism in the great cities.'' [7] Such ''scientific benevolence'' was carefully distinguished by charitable organizations from the investigative activities of paid agents, on the one hand, and mere alms giving, on the other. According to Roy Lubove's exceptional historical analysis of the emergence of the social work profession, the first faint expressions of a professional self-concept and a professional mission for social workers were heard as early as 1893. The historical origins of social work and social services, then, can be found in the early decades of the last century.[8]

The provision of social services, however, long remained the exclusive concern of private social welfare agencies. The earliest public assistance programs enacted in the United States did not include any provisions concerning social services. The original enactment of the Federal Social Security Act of 1935 neither required nor authorized the provision of any social services. The only exception to this was an authorization under one of the titles which enabled states to voluntarily establish small child welfare services units. But these were organizationally separate and otherwise distinct from the financial assistance programs. Thus, for the ten to fifteen years following the 1935 act there remained very little relationship between programs of public assistance and the provision of social services.

The first major convergence of financial assistance provisions with social services occurred as a result of the 1956 Social Security Act amendments. These amendments included what is termed *enabling legislation* whereby state officials could avail themselves of federal subvention in order to provide services to strengthen family life. Western State took advantage of this sub-vention in 1957, as did many other states. This was followed by a series of experimental service programs and demonstration projects within the context of the financial assistance programs. For the next several years, roughly between 1957 and 1962, provision of financial aid remained more or less distinct from social services. All this changed radically with the passage of the 1962 amendments.

The legislative initiatives reflected in the enabling laws of 1956 were strengthened in the 1962 amendments. Most impor-tantly, the 1962 changes stipulated that the provision of social services was to be a mandatory precondition for any states seek-ing federal grants-in-aid. Central to this stipulation was the requirement that all persons receiving categorical aid must pos-sess, in their case record, a social service plan. This plan was to be formulated and carried out by a social worker in collabo-ration with the client. Moreover, the social worker was to be a person separate from those previously responsible for investigat-ing the client's eligibility for financial assistance, individuals typically without professional social work training.

One result of these changes was that "public assistance" became synonymous with the provision of social services. That is, all of the front-line workers became social workers regard-less of their previous training. The only exceptions to this gen-eral rule were those social workers employed by specialized agencies, such as a probation department or adoptions agency, and the very small number of social workers with specialized case files in those few counties which had special units for child welfare services. In the vast majority of counties, the services included under the rubric of child welfare were handled by social workers with nonspecialized caseloads, who were respon-sible for determining eligibility for financial assistance as well. Northern and Southern Metropolitan Counties, where our re-search observations were conducted, were among the few coun-ties which maintained specialized units of social workers to pro-vide child welfare services. Such workers, who typically had professional training through a Masters of Social Work degree from a college or university, were assigned small caseloads of welfare clients so that they were free, having been relieved of the many time-consuming tasks involved in determining eligibility, to devote their time to intensive social service practice.

Beginning in 1968, a series of legislative changes at the federal and state levels of government led to some significant changes in the administration of the public welfare programs. These changes effected a separation of social services from the income maintenance tasks of welfare departments, those concerned with the provision of categorical financial assistance. They made provision of social services voluntary rather than mandatory for states seeking federal grants-in-aid under the relevant titles of the Social Security Act. Organizationally these changes entailed separation of income maintenance functions, now performed by people called eligibility workers, from social services, now provided by social workers. Despite these changes, however, social service tasks remain partially subsidized by federal monies, as determined by the cost-sharing formulas in the legislation.

With the advent of these changes, there has been an increasing emphasis on the provision of documentary evidence that the social workers at the county level have provided "hard" rather than "soft" social services. Hard services are considered to be those involving some tangible service or product; examples might include getting food, medical aid, or clothing for a family, getting them to see a psychiatrist, arranging for legal advice, and so on. Soft social services are considered to be those where the result of the social worker's intervention is relatively intangible; examples might include counseling the client about how to cope with daily problems more effectively, helping a family to better understand the nature of their relationships with one another, assisting a client "work through" their feelings of hostility or agression, and so forth. Records and reports are regularly reviewed by federal auditors who check to see if states and counties are meeting their obligations under the legislation.

Conflicting interpretations by the social workers of the applica-
bility and relevance of the distinction between hard and soft
social services represented one of the ongoing and continual
struggles in the welfare offices. This struggle, and its relevance
for understanding how the official records were constructed,
was at least partially responsible for stimulating the author's
research interests in the social processes of making and using
official information, even though an investigation of this was
not included in the original research plans.

The Formal Tasks of Child Welfare Services

Throughout this discussion the topic of our research interests
has been referred to as child welfare services. This is the phrase
used in the original 1935 legislation. Because of various legal
changes and modifications, however, such activities were not
officially termed "child welfare services" in the offices where
the research was conducted even though social workers used the
term among themselves, as well as several other terms. Hence,
our usage may represent a possible source of confusion without
further clarification.

The official titles of the activities observed during the research were varied. A distinction was made between those
workers handling welfare cases which had been officially adjudicated before assignment to the worker and those workers
handling cases which had not gone through any formal adjudication process. In the former instance the cases involved situations
in which custody of children had been taken away from the
parents in a prior court proceeding. The children in these cases
were officially referred to as "dependents" or "wards" of the
court. In the latter instance, no such formal assignment had
been made, although in many of them children were voluntarily
placed in a foster home or other institution. In a few cases referrals for court adjudication were made subsequently. As used

here, then, the phrase "child welfare services" is a more general category embracing both kinds of welfare cases.

The organizational distinction noted above did result in some important differences in the nature of the activities performed by social workers in the various offices. For example, the social workers handling adjudicated cases spent a considerable amount of their time either preparing for or making court appearances, whereas the others spent little time doing this. Yet the types of problems encountered by both groups of social workers in their daily social casework were substantially the same. In both instances there were relatively few cases where the problem was considered to be child battery or sexual molestation. The vast majority of cases fell into the more ambiguously defined area "emotional neglect."

The five social welfare offices included in the research possessed some common features. In four of the offices there were two units engaged in providing specialized child welfare services; in the other office, there were three such units. Each unit consisted of five or six social workers and a social work supervisor. All of these units were located in large district offices housing between 250 and 400 other employees.

At these district offices, the CWS units constituted only a small portion of the total social services staff, and the entire social services staff typically made up slightly less than half of the total number of employees, with the majority comprising income-maintenance, clerical, and administrative personnel. As noted before, one feature distinguishing the CWS staff from other social services staff was the smaller client caseloads. The nature and size of one's caseload were specified by law. The social workers commonly referred to the legally mandated number of cases in a full caseload as the yardstick number. For the child welfare services social workers at the Metro office this number was twenty-five, whereas the number for social workers not in CWS was sixty. Typically, though, both groups of workers had more cases than this in their caseload at any one time, and the yardstick criteria also changed from time to time.

Since most of the research observations were conducted at the Metro office in Southern Metropolitan County, the following sections will present a brief overview of the formal tasks of CWS social workers at this office.

Child Welfare Services at the Metro Office

As we noted before, the responsibilities of the child welfare services units at the Metro office included the provision of social services to welfare clients who had not been involved, prior to referral to CWS, in an adjudication process pertaining to the custody of the children in the family. Some clients, however, had been previously involved in such proceedings, and in a few cases the CWS workers had initiated such adjudication when they felt it was warranted. In Southern Metropolitan County, these adjudicated cases were handled by the County Probation Department. The fact that a case had been adjudicated, however, affected only its legal/organizational status, not the nature of the problems in the family or of the services involved in the casework.

At the Metro office, child welfare social services were distinguished as intake and continuing services. Unit one consisted of a social work supervisor and five continuing-service workers; unit two consisted of a supervisor and six workers, three of whom were continuing-service workers and three intake workers. Intake services involved screening clients to determine their need to receive child welfare services. The three CWS intake workers sometimes provided short-term services themselves; usually they transferred their intakes to the continuing-service workers for ongoing casework after they had initially investigated the problem in a given case. The cases handled by the continuing-service workers could originate from sources other than the intake unit, most notably from other units within the

Metro office. The majority of their cases, however, came from intake.

Continuing-services workers have more time to choose and carry out solutions to family problems referred to them by Intake. However, the first task of a continuing-services worker is often to conduct his or her own investigation concerning the facts of a situation. In many cases, it was just such an investigation which led the intake worker to refer the case to the continuing-services worker in the first place so that more time could be devoted to resolution of the problem than was available to the intake worker.

Responsibility for CWS intake rotated among the three intake workers at the Metro office, with each one having intake duty approximately one third of the time during the week. Being on duty entailed staying at one's desk to handle incoming phone calls. If an incoming call involved what appeared to be an emergency situation requiring crisis intervention, the CWS intake worker could leave the office to provide the necessary services. In that case, someone else would cover his intake duty while he was away. Yet while such events were not uncommon, they did not occur with great frequency.

Most of an intake worker's activity involved handling non-emergency incoming phone calls. These calls were highly varied in nature. They included a wide variety of requests for information, such as requests for referrals to other social agencies in the community and calls from other agencies. Those calls most relevant to the provision of social services were commonly termed "complaints," a term which implies the existence of a problem situation. Upon receiving a complaint the intake worker investigated to determine whether or not it was justified and, if so, what could or should be done about it.

A claim that a problem exists in a family which may affect the welfare of the children may come from a number of sources. The claim may originate from some member of the family or from a close friend, relative, or neighbor. The majority of such complaints originate with other official agencies—the primary source at the Metro office being the social service workers in other units. Other sources include the police, probation authorities, schools, hospitals, public health nurses, community mental health clinics, and private agencies.

The determination of the nature of a problem and of the possible remedies for it is highly problematic. The "definitions" of social welfare problems contained in the various sets of formally codified rules, regulations, and procedures are largely irrelevant to the everyday tasks of the intake worker. In some cases workers don't know what the rules are; in other cases they may recall having previously reviewed them but are no longer quite sure what they say. Those social workers who routinely consult the officially codified rules in order to construct official documents (especially those related to court proceedings) are typically the most emphatic in commenting on the irrelevance of such regulations to their everyday work.

The statutory definitions are, from the social workers' point of view, far too abstract and general.[9] The determination of the nature of a problem in a particular case necessarily requires the intake worker to make use of his common-sense understandings of the motives and intentions of the people with whom he deals. Accordingly, the social worker's perceptions of the situational contingencies are assigned an overwhelming priority as a basis for making requisite decisions. One supervisor reflected as follows on the place of formal rules:

> All the manuals, the bulletins, rules, regulations, instructions, all of it, the whole bureaucratic mess of it, it's all for the Grand Juries and Board of Supervisors. . . . All these (pointing to the manuals in his office) gather dust most of the time. It's possible to go for years around here without even ever referring to any of them. They're just pulled off the shelves, the dust is blown off when we know that some members of the Grand Jury will be coming through the office for a visit, or when the Supervisors are on the rampage to "clean up welfare" or whatever it is at the

time. But all the bureaucratic paraphernalia is just show. It's just for show, really.

The kinds of practical actions which an intake worker may judge to be warranted in a given situation are numerous. The actions most frequently taken are referring to other agencies, providing some kind of short-term services, making a foster-home placement of a child, or referring the case to a continuing-services worker for more intensive work.

Placement in a foster home may be made either by an intake worker or by a continuing services worker. All such placements at the Metro office are of a "voluntary" nature, officially at least. On some occasions, an intake worker may create a new, or unofficial, foster home to meet the exigencies of a particular situation.[10] Owing to the vast amount of time required for the intake screening process, the three intake workers were assigned reduced caseloads, in that they provided continuing services for approximately ten to twelve cases as compared with twenty-five to thirty for the continuing-services workers.

Public Welfare: The Increasing Importance of Official Records

I have already noted that one of the results of the 1962 amendments to the Social Security Act was that public welfare became synonymous with the provision of social services. Another result was perhaps even more consequential: the federal regulations requiring formulation of a social service plan for each individual welfare client necessitated the development of a vast administrative network to handle the immense record keeping needed to provide documentary evidence that the state, county, and district offices were in fact living up to their obligations. This elaborate record-keeping apparatus not only required more time and effort on the part of those already involved, but also necessitated the allotment of additional financial resources and personnel to protect the state and county against federal audits.

One of the CWS supervisors at the Metro office, who had been involved in public welfare programs since the late twenties and had lived through all of the legislative and administrative changes discussed previously, offered these observations on the impact of these recent changes:

Supervisor: When I started out there was one person per county, the County Agent. Sometimes an agent would cover even more than one county. He alone was responsible for distributing thousands of dollars worth of food and other things to the needy. Back in [a large Midwestern city] everybody knew that of course the County Agent only handed out food for votes, or other favors sometimes, but we didn't have any paperwork at all then, at least not like we do today, so he could get by with it. It was a little on the shady side, everybody knew it, and I doubt if there was as much waste back then as there is now in the Commodity or Food Stamp programs, [which are] ensnarled in bureaucratic red tape so much that we probably waste more food than [is] given out to those who really need it. Now we have to justify everything we do on paper.

Myself: How much has it changed supervising? I mean, ten years ago did you. . . .

Supervisor: Well, it's changed a lot in some respects, in others perhaps not so much. At [another office within the same county] when I first began as a supervisor I spent much more time than I do now on actual case conferences. Now I spend most of my time filling out paperwork. That may have been because it was new to me then, though. I think, really though, that the paperwork mill has become a disaster. I can't even keep up with it myself anymore. Half the time I'm not sure what I've just signed.

Generally, the major overall impact of the recording and reporting requirements was the development of a close association between the daily work of the social workers and the perceived necessity for documenting this work. The connection was succinctly expressed in a department memo distributed to the CWS social workers at Metro during the research observations. Entitled "Services Recording and Supervisory Responsibility," the memo noted:

> Recording, for auditing purposes, serves as a means of accounting for our services program. Federal participation in the cost of the services program depends upon services provided and documented. Services are being given, but, for auditing purposes, if service reporting is inadequate, service has not been given. Remember, "If you didn't say it, you didn't do it." The first-line supervisor is directly responsible to proper services recording. Auditors, whether agency, state, or federal, only read the recording and report findings.

Recording requirements frequently served to reverse what one might think to be the expected relationship between the actual social service activities and the reports. That is, on many occasions the paperwork which documented provision of services became the social reality of primary importance, and the prospect of an impending record or report stimulated provision of service. Thus, an approaching deadline for completion of a report on one's actions often served as justification for a visit to the home of a welfare client even though it was not necessary.

The official records and reports were, as seen and used from the social worker's perspective, an effective public "front" for their everyday operations. One CWS worker commented:

> Christ, we really don't have [any] idea of what we're doing. We can't even agree on what we're supposed to do! Seems like we're fallin' on our face half the time, just wallowing around, sometimes falling all over each other, and always wondering what in the hell to do. But we never say that publicly, of course. Publicly, at least, all our efforts always fit nice and neatly in the classifications on [the recording form]. Yeah, the forms are always neat; it's always this or that, and it's never in between.

Another worker remarked, in reference to some statistical reports recently completed by the Probation Department—statistics which presumably gave some evidence of their work performance:

> [The Probation Department] does the statistics thing the same way we do here. Shit, you ought to know by now that it isn't what you actually do that makes a goddam bit of difference around here, but only what you *appear* to be doing. That's where it's at, just the numbers. They just say what you want 'em to say.

Finally, the worker in charge of the Foster Homes Licensing section concluded a CWS training session with the following plea to his fellow workers:

> Give me a call even if you know [what foster homes] are available. Don't sit on your duff if you think you already know the status [at Foster Homes Licensing]. The only way we're ever gonna get any more foster homes is if I can show the need for it. I need the calls for my statistics. That's the only way we'll ever get any more [foster homes], so please keep the calls comin' in even if you know nothing's available.

The number of records, reports, and other kinds of documentary evidence required appeared to increase even during the course of the research observations. Indeed, the increasing necessity for the state to prove to federal auditors via various forms of documents that it is indeed offering specific (or hard) social services has generated continuing conflict both in Western State and throughout the U.S. In the Metro office, the increasing emphasis on program and employee accountability had, in a few cases, reached the point where the opposite effect was occasionally produced. One of the CWS supervisors made the following comments as she affixed her signature to a mountain of various papers:

> I really can't keep up with all of this anymore. I think I've become somewhat numbed to all of the paperwork a supervisor is supposed to keep on top of around here. I'm getting so I'll put my signature on just about anything. I think everybody's in the same boat at the moment. Most social workers will do anything to save their jobs. I used to be very careful about most of this [in-

dicating the paperwork] 'cause I thought it was being used to make staffing decisions and budget decisions. But I don't think it makes much difference really. If the administrators want to justify some decision, then they'll change the reports. I've seen this happen all too often around here.

The substantive discussion of the research observations, findings, and analyses examines these phenomena in much greater detail.[11] The argument concerning the uses of official information is that in some respects such phenomena have been noted by many different observers over the last hundred years, while in other respects, contemporary activities relating to official documentation represent new and distinctive realities. At any rate, the ongoing dialectic between people work and paperwork dominated the everyday reality of the social welfare settings observed during the research project, and this tension concerns us throughout the remaining chapters.

While the purpose of this chapter was to present the reader with an overview of the settings studied during the research, and to provide a flavor of the daily activities occurring there, this background information is not extraneous to the following chapters. Unlike the many sociological field research studies of deviant groups, where the observer reports the members' impressive cooperation with him in the hope that he will tell their story to the hostile, outside world, few of the social workers with whom I studied were openly solicitous of any such public relations effect. Indeed, on several occasions, as we will learn in greater detail later, I was instructed in unequivocal terms that "telling the story" is not a universally shared value.

NOTES

1. Many others have ably provided such. To cite just a few of the excellent historical and sociological works concerning social welfare, see: Harold L. Wilensky and Charles N. Lebeaux, *Industrial Society and Social Welfare*. New York: The Free Press, 1965;

Jacobus ten Broek, ed., *The Law of the Poor*. San Francisco: Chandler, 1966; Roy Lubove, *The Professional Altruist*. New York: Atheneum, 1969; Anthony M. Platt, *The Child Savers*. Chicago: The University of Chicago Press, 1970.

2. Pseudonyms will be used throughout this report to mask the identification of actual settings, and to maintain the anonymity of those who made the investigations possible. The pseudonyms used to depict the various settings are Western State, Northern Metropolitan County Department of Public Welfare (and the offices herein referred to as Lakeside, Vandalia, and San Cristobal), Southern Metropolitan County Department of Public Welfare (and the offices herein called Metro and Bayside). When references are made to actual welfare cases or actual official records or reports, these will also be disguised by pseudonyms.

3. The characterizations in quotation marks are taken from *Time* magazine (December 28, 1970 and February 8, 1971), *Saturday Review* magazine (May 23, 1970), *U.S. News & World Report* magazine (February 8, 1971 and August 9, 1971), *Newsweek* magazine (February 8, 1971), and *Atlantic* magazine (August, 1971).

4. The quotation is taken from Ronald Reagan's "Meeting the Challenge: A Responsible Program for Welfare and Medi-Cal Reform," a message transmitted to the California legislature on Wednesday, March 3, 1971.

5. Frances Fox Piven and Richard A. Cloward, *Regulating the Poor*. New York: Pantheon, 1970.

6. The actual program titles under the original 1935 legislation were worded in a slightly different fashion, but for the sake of clarity I have used the current program titles to avoid terminological confusion.

7. Lubove, *The Professional Altruist*, p. 41.

8. *Ibid.*

9. For example, the Western State Welfare Code defines child welfare services as activities serving "to provide protective services for children so as to insure that the rights of physical, mental, and moral welfare of children are not violated or threatened by their circumstances or environment." It does not specify those circum-

stances or environmental factors which should be regarded as potentially injurious, or describe how one might identify them.

10. One structural feature of such foster home placements should be noted. The costs for such a placement are subsidized only in those cases involving persons who are also welfare clients. All others (termed "01 cases") must pay for it. Since it is very rare that any family can afford such costs in addition to their regular expenses, this results in a near-equivalence between the terms "foster home placements" and "welfare recipients."

11. Reference is made to the author's "The Social Construction of Official Information."

Chapter 3

Gaining and Managing Entree in Field Research

IN THE WRITTEN WORK about participant observation research, one issue consistently addressed concerns the process by which permission is obtained for the research project from those whom an investigator seeks to study. (In the case of covert research, the issue is one of establishing the initial contacts.) There are two salient reasons why this is regarded as important. One of them is so obvious that it hardly needs to be stated; the other is not so obvious. First, the achievement of successful entree is a precondition for doing the research. Put simply, no entree, no research. A cursory review of the literature shows, however, that it is easier to state this simple reason than it is to accomplish the task. Published reports of researchers' entree experiences describe seemingly unlimited contingencies which may be encountered, ranging from being gleefully accepted to being thrown out on one's ear. But there is a more subtle reason why the matter of one's entrance to a research setting is seen as so important. This concerns the relationship between the initial entree to the setting and the validity of the data subsequently collected. The conditions under which an initial entree is negotiated may have important consequences for how the research is socially defined by the members of the setting. These social definitions will have a bearing on the extent to which the members trust a social researcher, and the existence of relations of trust between an observer and the members of a setting is essential to the production of an objective report, one which retains the integrity of the actor's perspective and its social context. The existing field research literature has very little to say about this subtle relevance of gaining entree. But this is the major reason why the issue continues to command our attention.

This chapter has three purposes. First, the treatment of gaining entree in the traditional social science literature will be reviewed. (Since the literature is extensive, it will not be possible to review it in detail.) The basic problems which researchers have encountered will be presented, and some proposed solutions will be mentioned. Several of the implicit assumptions behind the traditional arguments will be noted. Even though providing detailed specifications of a researcher's methodological procedures is considered fundamental to the distinction between scientific and common-sense modes of investigation, the argument of this chapter is that the traditional methodological accounts, and indeed all methodological accounts, necessarily involve common-sense elements.

The second purpose of the chapter is to present detailed ethnographic descriptions and analyses of how entree was achieved throughout the social welfare research project of the author. Finally, by comparing the traditional arguments with our materials, the implications of these issues for the conduct of participant observation research will be addressed.

The Traditional Conceptions of Gaining Entree in Field Research

Not only is success in gaining entree to a particular social setting—otherwise referred to as entry or access or, more idiom-

atically, "getting in"—an essential precondition for doing research, but the attempts to do so are fraught with many
uncertainties. Furthermore, these occur at that stage in the project when the field researcher is feeling most anxious and uncertain about his enterprise.

The traditional field research literature on gaining entree
points out that how one gains entree to a particular setting varies
according to the setting, depending on a variety of contingencies.[1] Not all of those who have attempted to gain entree
have been successful, and some field researchers have been
thrown out of the setting. For example, sociologists John Gullahorn and George Strauss made several attempts to study labor
union–management relations during the 1950s.[2] They reported
that several of the unions were initially suspicious of Gullahorn
because of a particular public position he had previously taken
with respect to labor union–management relations. One interna-
tional union was suspicious of Strauss because of the person
who had initially accompanied him to an initial meeting. Chris
Argyris is a sociologist who was interested in studying large organizations; he reported several attempts to gain entree which
failed.[3] His subsequent reflections on these failures led him to
believe that his original plan to do down-to-earth research had
overly emphasized the "down" and was interpreted as a lack of
respect for those from whom he requested permission. In preparing for the field research subsequently reported in *The Dynamics of Bureaucracy,* sociologist Peter Blau mentions that his
first attempt to gain entree to a federal employment agency was
an unsuccessful one.[4] Finally, anthropologist Stanley Diamond
has provided us with a detailed account of a field researcher
who, despite elaborate preparations for a long-term field research project in the provinces of Nigeria, was actually forced
out of a setting after several months of the project had been
completed.[5] There have probably been many more unsuccessful
attempts to gain entree for a field research project; these examples represent a few of the failures which have been reported.

When a field researcher prepares to begin a project, he faces another possibility which is probably more typical than rejection. This involves a false start, necessitating changes in the field researcher's initial plans. For example, sociologist Don Zimmerman reports on his first attempt to study at the Lakeside Office, one of the large offices of a Department of Public Welfare.[6] To gain entree, Zimmerman included a copy of his research proposal along with his request for permission to do the study. The administrators at the Lakeside office initially refused the request, saying that his proposed research interests didn't have any apparent practical implications which might be useful for them. He was later granted permission for the study when he rewrote his research proposal in a more practical vein.[7] William Whyte, the author of the classic field study *Street Corner Society,* has also reported several of the false starts of his research project.[8] One such now appears quite humorous, although it may not have been experienced as such by Whyte at the time.

He [a researcher giving advice to Whyte] also described how he would occasionally drop in on some drinking place in the area and strike up an acquaintance with a girl, buy her a drink, and then encourage her to tell him her life-story. He claimed that the women so encountered were appreciative of this opportunity and that it involved further obligation.

This approach seemed at least as plausible as anything I had been able to think of. I resolved to try it out. I picked on the Regal Hotel, which was on the edge of Cornerville. With some trepidation I climbed the stairs to the bar and entertainment area and looked around. There I encountered a situation for which my adviser had not prepared me. There were women present all right, but none of them was alone. Some were there in couples, and there were two or three pairs of women together. I pondered this situation briefly. I had little confidence in my skill at picking up one female, and it seemed inadvisable to tackle two at the same time. Still, I was determined not to admit defeat without a struggle. I looked around me again and now noticed a threesome: one man and two women. It occurred to me that here was a maldistribution of females which I might be able to rectify. I approached the group and opened with something like this: "Pardon me. Would you mind if I joined you?'' There was a moment of silence while the man stared at me. He then offered to throw me downstairs. I assured him that this would not be necessary and demonstrated as much by walking right out of there without any assistance.[9]

The nature of the problem faced in gaining entree appears to vary depending on whether the field researcher chooses to study a large-scale, formal organization, such as a welfare office, or a more open setting, such as a street-corner gang. The nature of the problem also depends on whether the field researcher chooses to do overt or covert research. Secret investigations involving large organizations tend to be rare. One example of such was the secret team research conducted by John Lofland and Robert Lejeune and their students on several Alcoholics Anonymous groups.[10] Perhaps the most famous example was Melville Dalton's research in several large corporations, reported in *Men Who Manage*.[11] Dalton writes that his decision to conduct secret research was based on his knowledge of others' prior experiences, including several occasions when social researchers were led down the garden path by those within an organization:

In no case did I make a formal approach to the top management of any of the firms to get approval or support for the research. Several times I have seen other researchers do this and have watched higher managers set the scene and limit the inquiry to specific areas—outside management proper—as though the [research] problem existed in a vacuum. The findings in some cases were then regarded as ''controlled experiments,'' which in final form made impressive reading. But the smiles and delighted manipulation of researchers by guarded personnel, the assessments made of researchers and their findings, and frequently trivial areas to which alerted and fearful officers guided the inquiry—all raised questions about who controlled the experiments. This approach was not suited for my purposes. Rather, by building on personal knowledge, I furthered the research through intimates— those who gave information and aid that, if generally known, would have jeopardized their careers. Though they knew of my general interest, I made no detailed statement of what I sought, and in all cases I indicated that my general interest was broad information on "all kinds of personnel problems" from as many firms as possible.[12]

The decision to conduct a secret investigation in which the researcher does not make known what he is doing obviously solves the problem of gaining entree to some extent. But such a decision does not guarantee that the members of the setting will trust the researcher and allow him access to valid information concerning their actions. A decision to conduct a secret investigation must necessarily be based upon the researcher's common-sense evaluation of whether or not such an investigation will be effective. This is not an easy thing to judge. One might suppose, for example, that secret research wouldn't be necessary in such a place as a public bureaucracy but might be called for in a study of a criminal group, presumably because the latter has things to hide from public awareness. However, there are several arguments which suggest the opposite. On the one hand, much of the traditional field research literature suggests that many of the most difficult problems in gaining entree occur in large bureaucratic organizations, including public or governmental agencies. On the other hand, in his excellent analysis of conducting field research among criminal groups, sociologist Ned Polsky argues that research among known criminals isn't as impossible as one might expect. He says that such persons often welcome researchers for what they hope will be the public-relations effect of the investigation, and they often desire to have their story told to the outside, "straight" world.[13]

Overt research in settings which are not as formally organized as public bureaucracies or business corporations, such as various deviant groups, street-corner gangs, or ethnic communities, is more common in sociology and anthropology than is secret research. Examples of such research would include Whyte's *Street Corner Society,* Herbert Gans's studies *The Urban Villagers* and *The Levittowners,* Eliot Liebow's *Talley's Corner,* Arthur Vidich and Joseph Bensman's *Small Town in Mass*

Society, Art Gallaher's *Plainville,* John Seeley, Alexander Sim, and Elizabeth Loosley's *Crestwood Heights,* and many others.[14] This type of research appears to differ from research in large-scale organizations in that successful entree for the research project is much more dependent on the field researcher's ability to establish successful rapport with a key leader in the community. When this occurs, the key leader will often shoulder some of the responsibility for seeing that others understand and accept the research project. Many of these researches don't involve a formal request as such for permission to conduct the research. Such a request would depend on the circumstances.

Adequate background work, delineation of the research problems, selection of a setting for the project, and a decision as between overt or covert research procedures are all matters which are, to some extent, addressed prior to the attempt to gain entree to a setting. This phase of a field research project might be termed preresearch research. The accomplishment of successful entree to the setting partially revolves around the field researcher's skill in explaining his initial interests in terms that make sense to the members of the setting. Implicit throughout the traditional literature on these problems is the message that what may be the researcher's theoretical problem is a decidedly practical matter for the members. Put differently, not only do the members want to know what the researcher is up to, but they also want some plausible rationale which might justify their cooperation. In short, What's in it for me? Rosalie Wax has addressed this problem:

> "Why should anybody in this group bother to talk to me? Why should this man take time out from his work, gambling, or pleasant loafing to answer my questions?" I suggest that as the field worker discovers the correct answers he will improve not only his technique in obtaining information but also his ability to evaluate it. I suggest, moreover, that the correct answers to these questions will tend to show that whether an informant likes, hates, or just doesn't give a hoot about the field worker, he will talk because he and the field worker are making an exchange, are con-

sciously or unconsciously giving each other something they both desire or need.[15]

This exchange model of human interaction, in which the information elicited by the field researcher represents a form of quid pro quo, is, of course, an oversimplification, and possibly a distortion. It overlooks the importance of existing relationships of power within a given social setting. It neglects the fact, for example, that some members may feel constrained to answer the researcher's questions, not because they're receiving some form of quid pro quo for their responses, but because some higher-ups have approved the research. On the other hand, it is rare that the relationship between the field researcher and the members of the setting involves dimensions of power. For the most part, the reciprocities exchanged between the field researcher and the members typically involve much more mundane matters. Rosalie Wax comments further on the nature of these reciprocities:

> The gifts with which a field worker repays the efforts of his informants will, of course, vary with each investigational situation. Some will be simple gifts like relieving boredom or loneliness. Others will be on a more complicated psychological level, like giving an informant who thinks himself wronged an opportunity to express his grievances. And, not infrequently, the field worker who comes to understand why an informant talks to him will not be particularly flattered by this knowledge.
>
> The fact that many informants talk freely because they are lonely or bored is perhaps not sufficiently appreciated by young field workers. Notebooks full of data may be acquired from an elderly person or from an individual who does not get along well in his community. The skill of an interviewer often plays a minor part in the accumulation of these data. The lonely informant has simply found someone who will listen to him.[16]

From these written accounts concerning the various problems encountered in gaining entree in field research, there emerges a paradox. On the one hand, it is commonly recognized that, as Burleigh Gardner and William Whyte note, one's research proposal must make sense to those empowered to grant or deny permission to the researcher to enter the setting.[17] On the other hand, many field researchers have recorded observations to the effect that their problems, interests, and questions commonly emerge only during the course of the research project itself.[18] With the exception of vague advice that one's research bargains or promises should remain flexible, none of the articles on field research explicitly describes how a particular investigator actually resolved this paradox. It is plausible to suggest that many researchers have promised what had to be promised in order to gain initial entree to the setting. In some cases, subsequent conflicts developed between the sponsor's previous understandings of these agreements and what emerged retrospectively as the researcher's ethical commitments.[19] A review of the traditional literature will provide few clues about how one might decide between the claims of practicality and morality. This could be taken as some kind of clue in itself.

The traditional accounts of gaining entree are many and varied. Taken together, they constitute a lode of anecdotes from which many nuggets of cultural wisdom may be mined. Throughout these works, however, there are a set of unexamined presuppositions—key ideas which are assumed to be true but are not subjected to analysis. First, all of the traditional articles about gaining entree assume that it is a purely practical, even technical, operation. Resolution of these dilemmas is not seen as requiring any theoretical understanding of the setting in question, nor is the solution to the problem considered to depend on the researcher's theoretical perspective. That this problem has been traditionally conceived of as a matter of technique is evidenced by all of the works previously referred to in this chapter. None of these argue that the definition or resolution of the problem is related to one's theoretical perspective. Second, all of these writings presuppose a common theory of rational decision making. When confronted with substantive problems involving decisions on which research bargains to make or which research role to select and play, the researcher is assumed to make a rational decision from among a number of possible alternatives prior to engaging in social interaction. Third, after a decision is made on a specific research problem, it is commonly assumed that the research situation remains stable and unchanging throughout its course.[20] Finally, whatever substantive particulars were reported about a given research project, it is assumed in each and every case that a solution to such problems is of a normative nature. The traditional literature is replete with vague prescriptions about "being a nice guy," "being open," "being honest," "being a regular guy," and so forth. Using these prescriptions is implicitly considered to open the magic door to the setting so as to obtain valid and reliable data in field research. Cunning, deception, or the use of power are never reported by field researchers as elements of their own actions. When these kinds of actions are mentioned at all, it is always implied that *others* engage in them.

The remainder of this chapter presents ethnographic materials describing how entree was gained and managed during our investigation into two metropolitan county departments of public welfare. These materials show that some of the traditional field research arguments are vastly oversimplified. Our analysis shows how entree strategies are related to one's theoretical understanding of "how a bureaucracy works." Furthermore, we claim that the model of rational decision making occasionally works in a fashion which is opposite to that indicated in the traditional writings. Finally, our materials document that what often emerges as a resolution of the entree problem is partially political in nature. If these arguments are correct, one implication is that all research conduct necessarily involves the observer's reliance on his common-sense understanding of society and of the nature of social interaction.

PRACTICAL STRATEGIES FOR GAINING AND MANAGING ENTREE

We have already mentioned the seemingly unresolved paradox about the problem of gaining entree. To restate this paradox: it is observed by many field researchers that the substantive focus of the research often emerges only after some portion of it has been completed, yet it is also observed that successful entree requires that the proposal make sense to those empowered to grant or deny permission for the project. To complicate this paradox, many who have done research in large-scale organizations have observed that one's research "cover story" may work at one level of the organization but not at another.[21] This raises the following question: how are social researchers to learn the practical organizational knowledge needed to gain official clearance for the research project and yet prevent premature disclosure of substantive interests? Any definitive answer to this question would necessarily entail a theory of formal organizations far surpassing the understanding one is presently able to glean from contemporary sociological literature on these topics. In the absence of such definitive knowledge, the following materials will depict the strategy and working theory that was used to accomplish successful entree at several social welfare agencies. Since such a written account necessarily emphasizes the amount of rational calculation involved in gaining entree, it is best to emphasize at the outset that "playing it by ear" is an essential, continuing component of this phase of social research.

OBTAINING INSIDE INFORMATION

According to standard methodology texts and the traditional literature on research, an investigator has an interest in some substantive problem and then plans a particular research project to pursue that interest. In actuality, however, the reverse of this is more common; hopeful investigators seek out some topic or setting which appears researchable and then develop an interest from there. At the beginning of this research project, an investigation of social welfare agencies was just one of several possibilities considered. For reasons which won't be elaborated here, other ideas for conducting a research project of a professional baseball team, a college sociology department, and United States Navy lawyers did not appear practical. The reasons behind the decision to conduct a research investigation of child welfare services social workers were preeminently practical in nature: (1) there was an inside informant in one welfare agency who was a close friend of one of the faculty sponsors of the research project; (2) I had previous acquaintances among social workers; (3) the office in which I desired to conduct the major portion of the unfunded research was close to my residence; and (4) my wife was then employed as a social worker in the Adoptions Agency of the same community. This subsequently turned out to be a critical feature of the initial entree at the Metro office, although I did not fully anticipate or appreciate it at the time.

Given the researchability of these social welfare settings, the initial ideas for the project were formulated in general terms. As mentioned earlier, the initial research interest was formulated vaguely as: how do social workers make a social welfare agency work? [22] As initially conceived, the primary focus of the research investigation was on the nature of the everyday, face-to-face interactions between social workers and welfare clients. The initial hope was to produce an ethnographic case study of social work practice. It was also hoped that such an ethnographic description would directly or indirectly provide a truthful understanding of how official agencies of social control actually operate.

As originally conceived, the research project was planned to include: (1) informal, tape-recorded interviews between the inside informant and her colleagues on the nature of their everyday work, (2) systematic participant observation by the researcher in the welfare offices with units of social workers performing child welfare services, (3) tape recordings between the researcher and the social workers taken before, during, and after their home visits, (4) transcribed recordings shown to other social workers in different offices for the purose of comparison and independent verification of shared meanings and common properties of social work practice, and (5) observations of the construction and use of the records collected within a given social welfare office. These plans changed throughout the course of the research. Some were not carried out as originally conceived, and others were added; but these were the initial ideas developed before the first efforts were made to gain entree to the welfare offices.

The original ideas for the investigation were not conceived of completely in the abstract. They were developed over several months of listening to some of the tape-recorded interviews conducted by the insider informant with her colleagues. From these interviews, it was learned that many of those in the Lakeside Office made linguistic distinctions such as punitive vs. supportive workers, administration-oriented vs. social service–oriented workers, liberals vs. conservatives, and strict rule interpreters vs. loose rule interpreters. From the existence of such distinctions a working theory was developed, though ambiguously articulated at the time, for the purpose of gaining initial entree. The gist of this working theory was that the formal schema of rules and regulations in the organization could be invoked by many variously situated persons for a diversity of reasons, none of which were necessarily related to any others. This suggested that it would be wise to use entree strategies which were as open-ended and unspecific as possible.

While the organizational knowledge developed from tape-recorded interviews proved to be invaluable for developing entree strategy, the tapes provided little of the tacit knowledge used by the members to order the setting. As my notes for the first day in the field recorded:

> I began my field research at the Lakeside office today and arrived there about fifteen minutes early, which was quite fortunate, because I became aware of one of the things which my inside informant forgot to tell me, namely, where to find a parking place. I arrived at the office sharply at eight o'clock, and, well, I guess I should've known better . . . I was the only one there!

Another example of tacit knowledge used by the members is taken from the notes for the first week of observations at the Metro office:

I arrived at the office a little before eight this morning. I saw Bonnie sitting at her desk reading the paper, and, since Frank hadn't arrived at his desk yet, I thought I would go over and have a short conversation with her. I walked over and sat down in Frank's chair, turned around, and said "Good morning," or at least I think that's what I said. Bonnie greeted this salutation with an icy stare and didn't say a word. After pausing for what seemed to be an eternity, I think I then shriveled up and slithered into my shoes seeking a place to hide. Shortly after this, Eddie told me that one of the unwritten rules of the office was that nobody was supposed to speak to Bonnie before eight-thirty in the morning.

The information obtained from tape-recorded interviews, then, provided limited knowledge of the inner workings of the organization.

USING A PROGRESSIVE ENTREE STRATEGY

Initial access to the Lakeside office was accomplished by means of a three-stage strategy of progressive entree.[23] The first stage involved a minimum request of the welfare officials of the Lakeside office: the insider informant asked for permission to interview her colleagues during their off-duty hours as an aid to a larger research project in social welfare. The second stage involved a request for the field observer to accompany the social workers during their everyday work activities. The third stage was a request for permission to take tape recorders along as part of the investigation. These stages were accomplished through what the members of the organization called "walking through" a request; that is, the request was made and granted in a face-to-face interaction.

There were several reasons for such an approach. First, another field researcher had reported considerable difficulty in making his initial research request and design acceptable to the Lakeside office. It was hoped this approach would avoid the requirement of formulating a research design, as well as premature closure of the research.[24] Second, the inside informant felt that administrative officials would regard the request for the use of tape recorders with suspicion, so this request was made subsequent to the first two. If it were denied, the research project would not completely die because of this one request. Third, official entree to this first office was judged to be an important "dry run" with respect to future plans to gain entree to the Metro office, where the field researcher desired to spend most of his time as a participant observer. The "dry run" strategy was used to concoct the appearance of experience on the part of the researcher. This proved to be much more important to the officials of the Metro office than was originally anticipated. Such constructions of experience are most relevant to those field researchers who are unable to convincingly present the powerful symbols of academic respectability as part of their credentials. A recent article by experienced field researcher Blanche Geer suggests that those capable of presenting these symbols convincingly may not necessarily be confronted with an entree problem.[25]

In one sense, all entrees are progressive in that a researcher gets to know more and more people as his research proceeds. In the case of the analysis here, however, the meaning of progressive entree is more limited. It refers to the field researcher's gradually increased requests for more open access to the insider understandings.

USING THE RHETORIC OF SCIENCE AND THE SYMBOLS OF ACADEMIC RESPECTABILITY TO CONSTRUCT A COVER STORY

Although it is seldom mentioned in field research literature, most field researches done in large-scale organizations have started with submission of either a research proposal or, at least, a letter of introduction. There are a couple of field researchers who report that their proposals were rejected or revised, or that the social meaning of their initial request was reinterpreted in light of new circumstances. But there is no mention of how such initial efforts are originally constructed.[26] Given the pervasive concern in the literature with the researcher's initial promises to those whom he seeks to study, it is reasonable to speculate that many field research efforts start through use of the powerful symbols of scientific or academic respectability. There are some who would argue that the use of such devices, like the choice of an open-ended entree strategy, is a necessity. Sociologist W. Richard Scott argues, however, that problems have arisen in the past because field researchers have shown a tendency to over-use such rhetorical devices in selling their research projects to organizational sponsors.[27] Perhaps this is what led the famous literary critic Kenneth Burke to observe several decades ago that social scientists tend to shape the ironies of everyday life to fit their own purposes and methodologies.[28]

In my efforts to gain initial entree to the Lakeside and Metro offices, I wrote and used two similar letters of introduction to the administrative officials of the two county departments of public welfare. Drafts of these letters were edited by several insider informants in the respective organizations. The rhetoric of science was used to persuade these officials to grant official clearance for the research. In addition, letterhead stationery from Western University and academic titles were used to lend academic respectability to both field researcher and faculty sponsor, and phrases such as "dedicated young scholar" and "reliable and trustworthy" were used in the letters.

DEFOCUSING FIELD RESEARCH

These letters of introduction were used as a part of a general strategy to "defocus" the field research. Brief comments indicated the general substantive interests of the researcher, but the wording was left as open-ended as possible. It was felt that such a letter possessed distinct advantages over a longer and more detailed proposal which could provide ammunition for any member who might choose to invoke organizational rules to reject it. (This appeared to have been the case in Zimmerman's field research.[29]) In my two letters, the general purposes of the research were presented as follows:

Although still in the formative stages, the primary research interests involve various family-related problems which social workers in Child Welfare Services deal with on a day-to-day basis, the kinds of problems and kinds of people with which they necessarily come in contact as a matter of their everyday work, the nature of the social casework involved in the handling of such cases, and some of the practical and/or legal constraints which the workers face in their jobs. Also, another interest in this research is the systematic elaboration of the methods of participant-observation.

This letter was used for two reasons. First, it "defocused" the research by allowing a wide latitude for study of the full range of organizational activities, of which the researcher was necessarily ignorant at the time the research design was constructed. Second, it provided greater freedom to negotiate the purposes of the research at each level of the organization, where the variously situated members could interpret the meaning of the letter in terms of their own particular concerns.

In summary, the initial letter of introduction stated the research purposes in general terms and used a minimum request for clearance. After clearance, it was possible to tender other requests for additional clearances and information. The viability of this strategy was noted by the assistant director of the county in which the Metro office was located. She stated that, from her previous experience, rejections of research proposals occurred at the point of initial contact with the agency. Subsequent requests were rarely denied when the researcher had already gained an initial clearance, or when research was already in progress.

NEGOTIATING INITIAL ENTREE:
   PLAYING BOTH SIDES AGAINST
   THE MIDDLE

At the Lakeside office, where the research began, the first, minimum request was "walked through" to the office of the director by the inside informant. Subsequent requests were made and granted for the field researcher to observe the activities of the social workers in their actual settings. This was followed by a request for permission to take a tape recorder. These early events were seen as important in that the researcher was able to present himself as experienced when he attempted entree to the Metro office, one known to possess far less "research maturity," as it is euphemistically termed in the traditional literature.[30]

In the second county where research was conducted, the assistant director of the Department of Public Welfare called me to her office to discuss the letter of introduction. As a prelude to this conference I went to the Metro office, where I wanted to conduct the field research, and discussed the project informally with the social work supervisor of one of the two CWS units. While the supervisor appeared to find the ideas for my research interesting, he suspected that one of my reasons for talking with him was to make it possible for me to report to the assistant director that the plans for my research had already received the unofficial approval of the first-line supervisors. During our talk, the supervisor wanted to know how far I had gone in trying to have the research approved. When he discovered that I was scheduled to talk to the assistant director that afternoon, he enjoined me not to mention our conversation; he said his name could not be used to tell the assistant director that the project had already been approved by the first-line supervisors. After many months of field research I learned that the organizational members refer to the strategy I had been using as "playing both sides against the middle."

If such a phenomenon were viewed in the framework of the common-sense model of rational decision-making promoted by the traditional field research literature, it would be considered one of the rational choices made by a researcher from among a list of alternatives available prior to gaining entree. From the above illustration, however, it is evident that such a model represents a fundamental distortion of what actually occurred; it was only *after* playing both sides against the middle that it was learned what had happened. The result occurred before "the decision." The decision to play both sides against the middle is more truthfully understood as the product of the search to understand, retrospectively, what has actually occurred.

During the initial conversation with the assistant director, two features seemed to be decisive in winning her approval: (1) the researcher had experience in doing this kind of work; and (2) the request for long-term participant observation was merely one portion of a larger research project. After several months of research, many of the social workers in the Metro office made comments to the effect that their department often followed the lead of the county to the north, where the Lakeside office was located. The frequent association of the research observations at Metro with those made at the first county was one of the devices most commonly used by the members, as well as myself, to legitimize the research activities. In discussing the letter of introduction, the assistant director expressed her surprise that the research included full-time observations for a period of six to nine months. After raising a number of questions regarding this seemingly extensive length of time, she commented that it would be necessary for her to clear the request personally with the director of the Department of Public Welfare. She then picked up the telephone, called the director, and informed him that a doctoral candidate from Western University had requested permission to do research at the Metro office for either one morning or one afternoon per week for a period of six to nine months. At the conclusion of this call, made in my presence, I reiterated to the assistant director that I desired to work full-time, rather than one morning or one afternoon per week. She replied that she understood the initial request correctly, but that, because of the unusual nature of the request, it would undoubtedly be denied by the director if he were to understand that the research required a full six to nine months. When asked what should be said to the various supervisory officials and social workers at the Metro office, she replied that she would send a memorandum to the people at Metro and inform them that the research project had been officially cleared for full-time observation.

In this last example of playing both sides against the middle, it can be seen that the workability of this strategy is enhanced by the technological superiority of the telephone over written communications with respect to the speed with which messages can be communicated and consent negotiated. The above examples also document a notion widely shared by many of the members, that verbal communications possess a potential for subsequent renegotiation to a much greater extent than do written communications, such as research designs. However, this characteristic does depend on the speed with which decisions are made within a given setting.[31]

During our conversation, the assistant director expressed only superficial concern with the theoretical and substantive interests of the research project. Her concerns revolved around broad political and legal issues that could be raised. She interpreted my initial letter of introduction in terms of the problems that could result if the researcher failed to observe the formal rules and regulations of the agency. She wanted reassurance that (1) the observer would maintain the anonymity of all department employees and welfare clients in any written materials which might result from the research, and (2) the observer would honor the legal strictures guarding the confidentiality of welfare clients, so that none of the welfare clients would be identified in the research nor any information about them used for purposes other than the administration of public assistance. The assistant director expressed only a passing concern about the extent to which the observer would interfere with the everyday routines of the social workers; she appeared satisfied with my comments that I would endeavor to keep interference to the minimum.

NEGOTIATING THE INITIAL ENTREE
DOWN THE LINE

When initial entree was subsequently renegotiated at the district level of the organization, potential political or legal ramifications were not mentioned at all. In subsequent conversations, the research request was related to the everyday practical problems faced by persons at those levels.

After the conversation with the assistant director, there was a meeting with the assistant district chief of the Metro office. This man expressed greater substantive interest in the proposed research project. He asked many questions related to my theoretical orientation and particular concerns. He was specifically concerned with how the theoretical and substantive interests could possibly be related to what the social workers in the CWS units were doing. He suggested the possibility that the observer might be misguided in his desire to pursue these interests at this particular office. Also, he was more familiar with the everyday working routines of the social workers. He requested more information than the assistant director about how the observer planned to conduct the field research so as to minimize interference with workers' everyday activities.

At this level of the organization, persons with recent graduate-school training in the social sciences were encountered. They requested justification of particular substantive interests in terms of present literature in the social science disciplines with which they were most familiar. In retrospect, it appears that the strategy used to confront these situations could be called "playing it by the seat of one's pants." As the audience reviews of these performances emerged several months later, the notices were mixed; but for the most part my performances were unconvincing.

The next stop at Metro included the first-line supervisors of the two CWS units. Here the letter of introduction was interpreted in terms of more practical and mundane considerations. The first-line supervisors wanted to know where the observer intended to sit, how the scheduling of visits with the social workers to welfare clients' homes would be arranged, and how the introductions to the clients would be made, and wanted more specific reassurances that the observations would not interfere with their workers' normal routines. The comments addressed to many of these concerns were generally directed toward reducing apprehensions by invoking the exception rule (i.e., asserting an exemption, for the research observations, for any topic that appeared to worry the workers). For example, one supervisor was especially concerned about my presence on home visits at which a social worker would make initial contact with the welfare client, a situation often experienced as particularly difficult by many workers. My response to this concern was that the field research would not necessarily require my presence in such situations. (It was possible, however, after relationships of trust had been established, months later, with several social workers in these units.) At the suggestion of the assistant district chief of the Metro office, the supervisors agreed to call a joint meeting of their respective units to give me an opportunity to explain the purposes of the research to their workers and to meet all of them in person.

The assistant district chief set a date for the meeting. When he informed me of this date, he said he would have to come to this meeting to make my introduction. In explanation he said that the supervisors of these units had a long-standing feud between them. If he were to allow either of them to make the introduction at a meeting at which workers from the other unit were present, it would give one of them the upper hand in this continuing struggle. During the three-day wait for this joint meeting, I read and reread Peter Blau's account of what I thought was a very comparable situation.[32] I prepared a brief outline of the comments I wished to make to the social workers.

MANAGING A "CRUCIFIXION"

Months later, I learned that some workers referred to this meeting as "the crucifixion." One worker called it "the donnybrook." As these terms suggest, I was never able to begin speaking from the notes I had drafted. After I was introduced by the assistant chief, but before I was able to make an opening comment, one of the social workers accused me of being a spy from the governor's office. He voiced his great displeasure with the assistant district chief, who was in the process of leaving the room, for his "treacherous complicity" in such a conspiracy. The worker demanded more detailed clarification of the situation. The assistant chief reiterated his previous comments to the effect that the request to do field research at Metro was indeed a legitimate research project sponsored by Western University. Then he turned the meeting over to me.

Even though detailed field notes of this meeting were recorded within a few hours of its termination, my recall of specific questions asked and answers given was very limited. Eight of the twelve persons in attendance had earned graduate degrees within the last five years, and some of them had concentrated on one of the stated purposes of the research, the investigation of the nature of social casework practice. They asked a series of specific questions regarding the prospective observer's knowledge of current literature in the field of social work. Fortunately, I had reviewed some of it in preparation for the research. However, both my own impressions of my performance at this meeting and the comments made by others several months later indicated that virtually none of those present found my explanations and comments convincing.

Two features emerged during this meeting which saved the proposed investigation from the fate of irreparable suspicion. First, the obvious surprise with which I greeted those accusing me of clandestine operations and my equally obvious lack of composure under fire while answering questions apparently constituted prima facie evidence that I was what I presented myself to be. As one of the members remarked months later, if a stranger really had been a spy from the governor's office, he would have been much more cool about it. Second, as the meeting neared its conclusion, one of the supervisors commented that she knew my wife was a social worker, had been previously employed in that very office, and was regarded highly by those within the office who knew her. This was a credential I had forgotten to use.

Of the factors which accounted for the social workers' initial suspicions of the research project, two seemed to be of crucial importance. The first involved the social workers' interpretations of my frequent use of the word "problematic" during the first meeting. When I would speak of the "problematics" of social casework or would use an example drawn from previous observations to indicate a "problematic" feature of social casework, many of the social workers apparently thought that I was trying to find out what was wrong with social welfare. Six months later, when there was a necessity for further clarification of the goals of the research, I tried to explain my use of the word. A recent article by field researcher Robert Habenstein documents similar difficulties encountered in the use of the word "problem." [33]

The second crucial factor contributing to initial suspicion of the research was the recent arrest of one of the social workers in Child Welfare. Though I was unaware of it at the time of the meeting, I later learned that the worker had been arrested, jailed, and, because of the costs of defense counsel, threatened with financial ruin. He had been performing his job in a fashion which had been standard operating procedure at Metro. After the arrest, several of the workers established a legal defense fund to aid their colleague and then found themselves viewed with suspicion by some of the administrative officials within the office. The proposed research, therefore, was suspected by some members as merely one more policing procedure to be used by the administration against the workers. During the initial meeting, one worker asked why this particular office had been selected from among the seven in the county. I responded by stating that this office happened to be the one closest to my residence. Several months later one of the social workers commented that many of them had found it difficult to believe that this office could have been selected by chance. Even though I thought I had made rather elaborate preparations before attempting entree at Metro, I was chagrined to learn that no information about the arrest had been obtained from the inside informants. This was certainly one of the most salient features of the setting at that point in time. Upon further reflection, however, I see that it may have been my own ignorance of this event which lent some credibility to my otherwise unpersuasive performance at that first meeting.

Not all of the social workers, however, were equally concerned about the spy allegations. Numerous questions were also raised about more mundane matters. Several of the workers described situations in which the introduction of a field researcher could unnecessarily interfere with interactions taking place. For example, one worker said she had several cases involving persons whom she described as man-haters, persons who were distrustful of men; she asked about the feasibility of allowing the field researcher to accompany her on visits to their homes. Upon reflection, I answered such questions by invoking the exception rule referred to earlier. Privately, I hoped to be able to accompany the workers on such calls after I had established relations of trust.

The reason that one of the terms later used to describe the meeting was "donnybrook" was not that the social workers formed a common front against me, the outsider; rather, the meeting, called to introduce the research, occasioned a heated argument between two of the social workers. It began when one of the workers asked how the researcher was to be introduced to welfare clients during home visits. I responded that the method of introduction really made no difference; I should be introduced in a manner which was most comfortable for each individual. I added that in the other three welfare offices I was introduced as a new social worker trying to learn the ropes. The social worker who asked this question not only expressed her surprise, but commented that such an introduction wasn't the right thing to do because it wasn't true. At this juncture, another worker rejoined that the issue at hand wasn't a matter of right and wrong but rather an issue of the most efficacious method for introducing the researcher with a minimum amount of discomfort to all parties involved. Thereupon ensued an intense discussion on the merits of introducing a researcher to welfare clients as a new social worker versus as a field researcher. There was no apparent consensus on the matter.

The initial entree, as subsequent materials document, did not result in a fixed state of affairs. It didn't open any magic doors. The initial entree was renegotiated and its social meaning reinterpreted on several different occasions. One of these occasions involved simultaneous changes in the positions of district chief and assistant chief, the two highest administrative positions at Metro. This changeover eventually led to an explicit renegotiation of the first research bargain with one of the assistants to the assistant chief. Another occasion for renegotiation arose as a result of the convergence of several complicated considerations, the precise nature of which I was never completely certain of. The most important consideration, I think, involved the social workers' changing evaluations of the potentially threatening features of the governor's proposed welfare reforms. I responded to these ambiguously defined feelings by constructing a fictitious outline of the final research report, my dissertation. This put many of the workers at ease. Another major renegotiation occurred during the tenth month of my residence at Metro. For reasons which were never too clear either to myself or to any of the other workers, one of the supervisors insisted that my research should be terminated. This supervisor tried to solicit complaints about the research from other workers, and appeals were made to the district chief and the assistant chief. All of these actions proved unsuccessful, but in the course of them the research bargains were, once again, renegotiated at all levels. On the basis of my own observations and reflections, and especially those of the CWS social workers, the most plausible explanation for these events was that I had become a pawn in the ongoing struggle between the two CWS supervisors.[34]

SUMMARY AND CONCLUSIONS

This chapter has been concerned with the problems of gaining entree to social settings for the purposes of social research. The chapter began by considering the major arguments found in the traditional field research literature of sociology and anthropology. Throughout this literature there is an implicit recognition that the nature of entree problems is partially dependent on the kind of setting chosen for the inquiry and the kind of research planned.

This chapter brings to light a series of assumptions that have been made about the problems and solutions of entree. The solution of this research problem is common-sensically conceived of throughout the traditional literature as involving the following elements. First, gaining entree is not thought to require any theoretical understanding of the setting prior to the research. Second, it is considered to involve various reciprocities, usually termed the research bargains or promises, which supposedly remain stable over time. Third, it is thought to involve, for the observer, a research role which also remains stable throughout the project. Finally, achieving entree is seen to depend on following such vaguely defined prescriptive rules as "being a nice guy," being honest, and so forth. Like all of the methodological writings in the social sciences, the traditional field-research literature assumes that providing an account of one's methodological procedures is what authorizes the research as "scientific" rather than common-sensical in nature. While it is not our intention to take the difference between science and common sense lightly, the materials in this chapter emphasize that gaining and managing entree in field research necessarily involves the use of an observer's common-sense knowledge, perceptions, and judgments.

This chapter shows that the traditional field-research literature has given us an oversimplified picture of the conduct of scientific research. The materials point out that a successful entree is not the beginning of a field research project, but rather follows a preresearch phase. During this phase, the investigator collects background information concerning how things typically work in a given setting. In this respect, the importance of contacts with inside sources of information cannot be overemphasized. The materials in this chapter also show, however, that even when such a preresearch inquiry is done, it may not provide the observer with the situationally specific tacit knowledge used by the members of the setting to organize their daily routines.

The existing field-research literature in sociology assumes that problems of gaining entree vary according to the type of setting chosen for study. In one recent volume, which includes analyses by thirteen well-known field researchers of the practices of their craft, it is argued that the problems one might encounter will vary depending on whether one wishes to study families, hospitals, labor unions, criminals, universities, and so on.[35] The materials presented in this chapter suggest that there are other factors of even greater importance, related not to the type of setting chosen for study but rather to the organizational members' interpretations of their circumstances. Such factors may include past experiences with social research and researchers or the present political climate.

Our analysis of traditional field-research literature recognized an unexamined paradox concerning the problem of gaining entree: namely, that one's proposed project must make sense to those empowered to grant or deny access to the setting, yet the foci of the investigation emerge only after some portion of the research has been accomplished. We argue that such a paradox is inevitable in a field-research project. The key to resolving the paradox, as presented in the ethnographic materials of this chapter, is the cover story, the claims made by an investigator in his research proposals and letters of introduction by which he legitimizes his request for access to the setting. The language of science as well as the powerful symbols of academic respectability are used rhetorically for this purpose. In this respect, then, the solution to the problem of entree in social research may be properly conceived of as political rather than normative in nature. We note that the cover story was only one step of a multistage "progressive entree" strategy. Such a strategy attempts to achieve access to the setting while minimizing premature closure of the research project by, among other things, "defocusing" the field research.

NOTES

1. There are many scholarly articles which have addressed these issues. Some of the better ones include: Robert K. Bain, "The Researcher's Role: A Case Study," *Human Organization,* 9 (1950): 23–8; Howard S. Becker, *Sociological Work,* Chicago: Aldine, 1970; Richard A. Berk and Joseph M. Adams, "Establishing Rapport with Deviant Groups," *Social Problems,* 18 (1970): 102–17; Peter M. Blau, *The Dynamics of Bureaucracy.* Chicago: The University of Chicago Press, 1963; Severyn T. Bruyn, *The Humanistic Perspective in Sociology.* Englewood Cliffs, N.J.: Prentice-Hall, 1966; W. Delany, "Some Field Notes on the Problem of Access in Organizational Research," *Administrative Science Quarterly,* 5 (1960): 448–57; Art Gallaher, Jr., "Plainsville: The Twice Studied Town," pp. 285–303 in Arthur Vidich, Joseph Bensman, and Maurice Stein, eds., *Reflections on Community Studies.* New York: Wiley, 1964; Joseph R. Gusfield, "Field Work Reciprocities in Studying a Social Movement," *Human Organization,* 14 (1955): 29–34; Robert L. Kahn and Floyd Mann, "Developing Research Partnerships," *Journal of Social Issues,* 8 (1952): 4–10; Stephen Richardson, "A Framework for Reporting Field Relations Experiences," *Human Organization,* 12 (1953): 31–7; William Foote Whyte, *Street Corner Society.* Chicago: The University of Chicago Press, 1943, 1955. Another excellent source is the collection of thirteen essays in Robert W. Habenstein, ed., *Pathways to Data.* Chicago: Aldine, 1970.

2. John Gullahorn and George Strauss, "The Field Worker in Union Research," *Human Organization,* 13 (1954): 28–32.

3. Chris Argyris, "Diagnosing Defenses Against the Outsider," *Journal of Social Issues,* 8 (1952): 24–34.

4. Blau, *op. cit.,* pp. 276–279.

5. Stanley Diamond, "Nigerian Discovery: The Politics of Field Work," pp. 119–54 in Vidich, et al., *op. cit.*

6. Don H. Zimmerman, "Paper Work and People Work." Unpublished PhD dissertation, Department of Sociology, University of California, Los Angeles, 1966.

7. Also see, Harwin L. Voss, "Pitfalls in Social Research: A Case Study," *The American Sociologist*, 1 (1966): 136–140.

8. Whyte, *op. cit.*

9. *Ibid.*, p. 289.

10. John F Lofland and Robert A. Lejeune, "Initial Interactions of Newcomers in Alcoholics Anonymous," *Social Problems*, 8 (1960): 102–11.

11. Melville Dalton, *Men Who Manage*. New York: Wiley, 1959.

12. *Ibid.*, p. 275.

13. See Ned Polsky, *Hustlers, Beats & Others*. Chicago: Aldine, 1967; Jack D. Douglas, ed. *Research on Deviance*. New York: Random House, 1972; and Carl B. Klockars, *The Professional Fence*. New York: The Free Press, 1974.

14. Herbert Gans, *The Urban Villiagers*, New York: The Free Press, 1962, and *The Levittowners*. New York: Random House, 1966; Art Gallaher, Jr., *Plainville*. New York: Columbia University Press, 1961; Eliot Liebow, *Talley's Corner*. Boston: Little, Brown, 1967; John Seeley, Alexander Sim, and Elizabeth Loosley, *Crestwood Heights*. New York: Wiley, 1963; Arthur Vidich and Joseph Bensman, *Small Town in Mass Society*. Princeton: Princeton University Press, 1958; and Whyte, *op. cit.*

15. Rosalie H. Wax, "Reciprocity as a Field Technique," *Human Organization*, 11 (1952): 34–7.

16. *Ibid.*

17. Burleigh B. Gardner and William F. Whyte, "Methods for the Study of Human Relations in Industry," *American Sociological Review*, 11 (1946): 506–12.

18. Among those who have noted this paradox of field research are: Howard S. Becker, Blanch Geer, and Everett Hughes, *Boys in White*. Chicago: The University of Chicago Press, 1961; Becker, *Sociological Work, op. cit.*, pp. 22–4; Anselm Strauss, *et al.*, *Psychiatric Ideologies and Institutions*. New York: Free Press, 1964, pp. 19–21; Kurt H. Wolff, "Surrender and Community Study," pp. 233–64 in Vidich, Bensman, and Stein, eds., *op. cit.*; Richardson, *op. cit.*, pp. 31–7; Whyte, *op. cit.*, p. 288; Blanch Geer, "Studying a College," pp. 81–98 in Habenstein, *op. cit.*

19. For an example of one such conflict, see Arthur Vidich and Joseph Bensman, "The Springdale Case: Academic Bureaucrats and Sensitive Townspeople," 313–50 in Vidich, Bensman, and Stein, eds., *op. cit.*

20. See, for example, Virginia L. Olesen and Elvi W. Whittaker, "Role-Making in Participant Observation: Processes in the Researcher-Actor Relationship," *Human Organization,* 26 (1967): 273–81.

21. See Bruyn, *op. cit.;* Geer, *op. cit.;* Kahn and Mann, *op. cit.*

22. The phrasing of the question here to some extent betrays the observer's perspective, the assumption being that a social welfare agency *does* "work" to the extent and degree that the members of the agency make it work. This assumption leaves open the question of *how efficiently* the agency works, which is a question for empirical investigation.

23. The idea of a progressive entree developed here differs significantly from the idea of a "double access" as developed by Kahn and Mann, *op. cit.* For the reader considering research in a hierarchically organized setting such as a large-scale bureaucracy, Kahn and Mann's idea of "double access" might be more appropriate.

24. See Zimmerman, *op. cit.*, Appendix.

25. Geer, *op. cit.*

26. See Blau, *op. cit.;* Diamond, *op. cit.;* Voss, *op. cit.;* Zimmerman, *op. cit.;* and many of the other references cited here as well.

27. W. Richard Scott, "Field Methods in the Study of Organizations," 272–82 in James G. March, ed., *Handbook of Organizations*. Chicago: Rand-McNally, 1962.

28. Kenneth Burke, *A Grammar of Motives*. Englewood Cliffs, N.J.: Prentice-Hall, 1950.

29. Zimmerman, *op. cit.*

30. Compare E. Jacobson, R. Kahn, F. C. Mann, and Nancy Moore, "Research in Functioning Organizations," *Journal of Social Issues,* 7 (1951): pp. 64–71.

31. This observation might apply, for example, only to those enterprises where the daily decision making moves at a relatively slow pace, such as welfare offices and universities. It might not apply to those settings, such as auctions or futures markets, where

the daily flow of decisions moves rapidly, where "taking some-one at his word" becomes a practical necessity.

32. See Blau, *op. cit.*, pp. 276–79.

33. Robert W. Habenstein, "Occupational Uptake," pp. 99–121 in Habenstein, *op. cit.*

34. A very similar situation occurred with a colleague of mine from the University of Illinois who was studying a welfare office in Delaware. After being on the scene for over a year, he was kicked out of the setting. He subsequently concluded that he had become a pawn in one of the interoffice political struggles.

35. See Habenstein, *op. cit.*

Chapter 4

Developing Trust

IF THE "OBJECTS" of social science knowledge were similar in nature to the objects investigated by the natural and physical sciences, then there would be every reason to hope that we could learn a great deal about human actions without ever leaving the relative quietude of the university laboratory. But this is not the case. The subject matter of the social sciences is fundamentally different from that of the natural and physical sciences. By understanding this, one recognizes the importance of one's participation in everyday life as a member of society. It is only participation in society which allows one to make sense of the activities routinely encountered in daily living. Commenting on this unique difference between the physical reality described by the natural scientist and the social reality described by the social scientist, the famous philosopher and sociologist Alfred Schutz writes:

> This state of affairs is founded on the fact that there is an essential difference in the structure of the thought objects of mental

constructs formed by the social sciences and those formed by the natural sciences. It is up to the natural scientist and to him alone to define, in accordance with the procedural rules of his science, his observational field, and to determine the facts, data, and events within it which are relevant to his problems or scientific purposes at hand. Neither are those facts and events pre-selected, nor is the observational field pre-interpreted. The world of nature, as explored by the natural scientist, does not "mean" anything to the molecules, atoms, and electrons therein. The observational field of the social scientist, however, namely the social reality, has a specific meaning and relevance structure for the human beings living, acting, and thinking therein. By a series of commonsense constructs they have pre-selected and pre-interpreted this world which they experience as the reality of their daily lives. It is these thought objects of theirs which determine their behavior by motivating it. The thought objects constructed by the social scientist, in order to grasp this social reality, have to be founded upon the thought objects constructed by the common-sense thinking of men, living their daily life within their social world.[1]

The social reality making up the observational field of the social scientist is not inherently objective in nature. It exists only insofar as it is interpreted as subjectively meaningful experience by living human beings. So it is only by some form of participation that it becomes possible to infer those meanings in actual settings of everyday life. Statistical measures of social existence are highly truncated accounts. They clearly do not speak for themselves, as some would have it; they require a perspective for their interpretation. Experimental techniques remove human activity from its natural setting and thereby distort it. Some could hope that experimental research might at least tell us something about the social meanings of experimental situations, but even that is doubtful. Survey and questionnaire researches involve preconceived and precoded categories originating from the observer's own common-sense perceptions; hence they do not remain true to the common-sense experiences of the members of society. Only observations involving participation with the members can get at the meaningful stuff of our common existence in the social world. While essential, however, it is this participation in the events being observed which leads to the problematics of field research. Schwartz and Schwartz have written:

> For our purposes we define participant observation as a process in which the observer's presence in a social situation is maintained for the purpose of scientific investigation. The observer is in a face-to-face relationship with the observed, and, by participating with them in their natural life setting, he gathers data. Thus, the observer is part of the context being observed, and he both modifies and is influenced by this context.[2]

Participation with the members of society in a particular context to fully understand the meanings of their actions is an essential ingredient of all valid observations. As noted above, however, participation always changes that context to some extent, always transforms that context into something other than its natural state. This fact raises what is without doubt the central problem of inference and proof in participant-observation research. Howard S. Becker has written:

> This raises an important question: to what degree is the informant's statement the same one he might give, either spontaneously or in answer to a question, in the absence of the observer? [3]

How the observer's participation in the observed interactions alters them and how the observer's presence in the situations changes the statements made by the participants are the central questions related to the objectivity of the data collected during a field-research project. The vast majority of the writings found in the traditional field-research literature address these crucial questions in one way or another. There is a widespread consensus among field researchers that the rapport or trust between the observer and the members is an essential ingredient for the production of valid, objective observations.

Why is rapport or trust so important in field research? Several answers can be found in the traditional field-research literature.

Some argue that the members may not fully understand the conduct of science or may have certain fears regarding such an endeavor. Others argue that responses given by members may not be truthful because persons have various things to hide, vested interests to protect, fears of public exposure, uncertainties concerning the consequences of public disclosure, and so on. Many think that by establishing relations involving trust between the observer and the individuals in a setting, the observer may eliminate such features from the research, reduce their influence to the extent it is possible, or at least make an assessment regarding the relations between such phenomena and the research observations. In the traditional field-research literature these concerns have been termed the problems of, among other things, trust, rapport, getting on good terms, establishing and maintaining satisfactory relationships, creating effective relationships, ensuring the cooperation of participants, and developing close relationships.

The following section reviews the traditional literature's major arguments about how one establishes trust in participant-observation research. The four major theories relating to this phenomenon will be presented. The analysis will point out certain taken-for-granted assumptions common to these four theories. Following this, the chapter presents ethnographic materials to describe the procedures actually used in the present research to develop relations of trust.

THE TRADITIONAL THEORIES OF
DEVELOPING TRUST

No utterance of dissent can be found in the traditional field-research literature about the crucial importance of good field relations between the observer and the members of a social setting. The universal consensus on this point stems from two obvious facts. What the observer will be allowed to see in the setting and the truthfulness of the statements made by the members will depend on (1) how they define him as a person, and (2) how the observer's role is socially defined by others in the setting. Only the development of relationships involving trust enables a field researcher to make an assessment of the accuracy and truthfulness of the observational data collected and the effects of the observer's presence on the observed situations.

Since the systematic study of the ongoing field-research project has not been considered important in the past, the literature contains few descriptions of the actual procedures used to develop trust in a given setting. What the traditional literature does contain are numerous assertions which pertain to the importance of being honest, being open, being a nice guy, being accepted, being a regular Joe, and so on. The great problem of taking such prescriptions seriously lies in the fact that it is never exactly specified just what it means to be "a good person," for example. With this general proviso in mind, the retrospective thoughts contained in the traditional literature do contain several different theories on how trust is actually developed in everyday life.

Over two decades ago anthropologist Rosalie Wax became one of the first field researchers to analyze the ingredients of good rapport. Wax argues for a kind of *exchange theory of trust,* wherein relations of trust are conceived as the outcome of a give-and-take exchange of reciprocities between a field researcher and the members of a social group. Good rapport is conceived as resulting from a situation in which both the observer and the member in the setting have something the other needs or wants. Trust presumably results from a kind of reciprocal exchange on the part of both parties. Wax argues:

> "Why should anybody in this group bother to talk to me? Why should this man take time out from his work, gambling, or pleasant loafing to answer my questions?" I suggest that as the field worker discovers the correct answers he will improve not only his technique in obtaining information but also his ability to evaluate it. I suggest moreover, that the correct answers to these questions will tend to show that whether an informant likes, hates, or just doesn't give a hoot about the field worker, he will talk because he

and the field worker are making an exchange, are consciously or unconsciously giving each other something they both desire or need.[4]

Another common-sense theory of developing trust differs significantly from the exchange theory promoted by Wax. It is one properly termed *the individual-morality theory of trust*. Several of the traditional field-research articles have mentioned it. John Dean argues:

A person becomes accepted as a participant observer more because of the kind of person he turns out to be in the eyes of the field contacts than because of what the research represents to them. Field contacts want to be reassured that the researcher worker is a "good guy" and can be trusted not to "do them dirt" with what he finds out. They do not usually want to understand the full rationale behind the study [italics in original].[5]

This argument is termed the individual-morality theory of trust because it centrally involves an ancient common-sense idea used in Western societies for purposes of making moral evaluations. Specifically, the theory assumes that an individual possesses a substantial self, certain essence-like qualities that remain stable and unchanging over time. These qualities are assumed to transcend all situational involvements and also to make for essentially good or essentially bad persons. Further procedural specifications concerning what one actually does when one does good are not forthcoming, nor is it suggested how one might deal with the possibility that another might not define these acts as good ones. It might also be noted that the individual morality in question here is implicitly a morality of *intentions*. That is, presumably questions of doing good are resolved by the observer's intention to do good. No mention is made of an assessment of the consequences for others within the setting of one's being a "good guy." Presumably the moral rules which define doing good are of such an absolute nature that use of them is implicitly conceived as a morally satisfactory end in itself.

A third common-sense theory of doing trust is similar to the above theory in that it has morally sanctionable features, but it is significantly different as well. This theory might be termed *adoption of a membership morality*. This stance involves moral decision-making on the part of the observer. But it is not merely the individual's intention to follow the moral decision made which is definitive of this stance. It is also a commitment to follow up such a decision if need be. Ned Polsky argues:

> If one is effectively to study adult criminals in their natural settings, he must make the moral decision that in some ways he will break the law himself. He need not be a "participant" observer and commit the criminal acts under study, yet he has to witness such acts or be taken into confidence about them and not blow the whistle. That is, the investigator has to decide that when necessary he will "obstruct justice" or have "guilty knowledge" or be an "accessory" before or after the fact, in the full legal sense of those terms. He will not be enabled to discern some vital aspects of criminal life-styles and subcultures unless he (1) makes such a moral decision, (2) makes the criminals believe him, and (3) convinces them of his ability to act in accord with his decision. That third point can sometimes be neglected with juvenile delinquents, for they know that a professional studying them is almost always exempt from police pressure to inform; but adult criminals have no such assurance, and hence are concerned to assess not merely the investigator's intentions but his ability to remain a "stand-up guy" under police questioning.[6]

As the comments by Polsky indicate, the key idea of this theory is that the observer will commit himself to do anything within reasonable limits to protect and maintain the integrity of the group membership. Polsky notes there is a certain gray area here which concerns what a given individual will judge to be reasonable. The boundaries of this area must be addressed from a given observer's moral perspective on what is acceptable. But, unlike the previous theory, Polsky's argument suggests that this moral stance might involve an observer in numerous acts which others would define as bad, immoral, or illegal. For Polsky, such actions might be acceptable if they served the predefined purpose of protecting the integrity of the membership and the setting. While Polsky refers to such a commitment as a moral decision, which it certainly is, it should also be pointed out that there is a substantial amount of practicality in such a research policy for those interested in doing field research.

The fourth theory of developing trust is not only different from the above three but also in conflict with them. This theory might be termed *the psychological-need theory*. According to the remarks of sociologist Chris Argyris presented below, obtaining valid and reliable data in field research does not involve such phenomena as being well liked, being accepted, and so on, and a research project may be hindered by such emotional ties between the observer and the members of the setting. He argues that the observational data will be valid only if the members define the research project itself as fulfilling their psychological needs:

> I doubt if the personal impact of the researcher can be a valid motivator for subjects. If the researcher could somehow be "all-loving" and well liked, the resultant emotional tie between himself and his subjects could easily bias their reports. If one has emotional ties with the researcher, one might tell him that which one feels is pleasing to him.
>
> The researcher is, therefore, left with the subject's perception of his research as the primary motivating factor in inducing them to report valid information. Thus the research itself must somehow be perceived as need-fulfilling. The subjects (management, employees, etc.) must perceive the research as helping them to gain something which they desire; to explore problems hitherto not understood and unsolved. They must feel that they are contributing to something whose completion will be quite satisfying to them.[7]

These four theories about trust in field research are obviously based on very different presuppositions and, when compared to one another, contradictory. Yet each has a certain sense of plausibility about it. This is to say that each of these theories is of a common-sense nature. In none of them are explicit procedural criteria provided to the reader so that the truth of the theory could be subjected to independent verification. Without having information to the contrary, one might sense that one or the other is true, but it is impossible to say for sure. With respect to the ethnographic materials to be presented in this chapter, we will see that it is possible to select out bits and pieces of material to support each of the theories. During the course of the welfare investigation, a wide variety of reciprocities entered into the personal relationships between me and the members at Metro and other offices. With respect to the moral stance promoted by Polsky about maintaining one's dramaturgical loyalty to those in the setting, there were occasions during this research project when I came into possession of guilty knowledge of various kinds. There were also occasions when I was an accessory to illegal actions. Such actions included individual manipulations of welfare eligibility records for purposes of financial gain, fabrications of various kinds of official records for the purposes of achieving one's immediate purposes, and even a couple of situations involving agency-wide subversions of legal statutes. There were activities clearly interpreted as efforts to be a "nice guy," and others were interpreted as fulfilling the "needs" of the individuals involved. In short, there is a certain sensible ring to each of the four theories presented above.

To say that each of the theories of developing trust in field research possesses a sensible ring, however, is not to suggest that the real truth is represented by some kind of synthesis of these theories. Indeed, in addition to the common-sense traditional field-research theories, the existing literature includes several other unexamined assumptions. First, in every case it is assumed that the operational practices of developing trust with the members of a particular social setting are motivationally impersonal. In different terms, it is assumed that whatever one does during a research investigation, his actions are not motivated by personal or subjective factors. Indeed, these are seen as the actions of Anyman. Second, also in every case, it is assumed that actions intending the establishment of good rapport with the

members are biographically transparent. There are two elements
of this assumption. First, the assumption is that developing relations of trust is not dependent on the observer's biographically
unique personal experiences. Second, it is also assumed that developing trust is not related to others' putative definitions of
the observer's sexual status, racial status, socioeconomic background, appearance, abilities, goals, and so on. Rather, the traditional literature implies that developing trusting relations is
like a technical skill, equally effective with all members of a
given setting independently of any personal characteristics and
independently of their variable feelings and responses toward
the observer. Again, when one is doing nice guy, the actions are
presumably those of Anyman.

The remainder of this chapter presents ethnographic materials
which describe selected features of the interactions taking place
between the social workers and myself during this investigation
of social welfare activities. These materials are available, it
should be emphasized, only because of the intentional decision
to make the field-research process itself a topic for study and
reflection. If this had not been done, it is likely I would have
produced a very idealized account of my reflections on the biography of the project, perhaps very similar to those which presently exist. My reflections and analyses of the social welfare
research experiences lead me to conclude that a field research
project is personal in three important ways. These will be specified in subsequent pages. One important implication of saying
that scientific research is of a personal nature is that it necessarily involves the observer's common-sense competencies as a
member of society. When one observes that the methodological
accounts of the traditional field-research literature possess a
"common-sense" character, this should not be taken to imply
that it is somehow possible to transcend or go beyond common
sense by simply making the research process itself a topic of inquiry. Insofar as scientific research includes any personal elements, it is impossible to provide an *absolutely* literal description of one's methodological procedures. But given this caveat,

it is still possible to enlighten our understanding of research conduct by making the procedures more explicit. This is the purpose of this chapter.

Early Thoughts about Trust

While my field-research experiences at the Metro office might suggest it was only after a series of problematic experiences that the crucial importance of trust became clear, this is not in fact true. I presumed that trusting relations would be necessary even before the project began. This presumption was not, however, founded on suspicion of human beings in general or social workers in particular. Previous personal experiences involved occasions where social workers were present and included mystical ceremonials, parties where illegal drugs were used, and other events commonly conceived of as at variance with public morality. These experiences provided forewarning that the public routines to be observed at the welfare offices would constitute but one slice of these members' experiences.

To the extent that efforts were made prior to the research to think about trust, they were largely confined to reflections on previous life experiences. Two of these experiences were of greatest importance. First, I knew that I wanted to avoid what had happened during a previous field-research effort I undertook to prepare a term paper for a course. Months after the effort I termed this phenomenon "the problem of following the path of least resistance." Long before conceiving this phrase, I was aware that the phenomenon had been a fundamental determinant of the observations.[8] Second, and most important, personal friends had commented during the last several years that I was a difficult person to get to know, that I tended to be very reserved and didn't talk much about myself. These reflections, combined with the suspicion that some degree of stigmatization could result from trying to establish relations of trust with workers in large organizations where the project originates with official clearance from those in authority, led to the development of a *strategy of identity spoilage*.[9] This strategy was conceived as a practical procedure for constructing the appearance of humility for the observer. With the exception of this notion, all the other thoughts on the issue of developing trust emerged during the field experiences.

Since the first encounter with the social workers at the Metro office (the crucifixion), I was worried about whether it would be possible to establish the relations of trust necessary for the field-research project. Worries and feelings of anxiety accompanied the first weeks in the field. I was not worrying about following the path of least resistance; rather, my initial concerns revolved around finding a path of least resistance.

While the notion appears naive in retrospect, during the first six weeks of the field research the construction of an index of trust was attempted. I began by compiling a list of variables considered at the time to be related to developing relations of trust. Some of these variables as originally conceived were "Worker allows observer to accompany on home visits to clients' homes," "Worker originates request for observer to accompany," "Worker asks observer to go have coffee," "Worker invites observer to join self or group for lunch," "Worker gives feedback to observer about how other workers are commenting on the research," "Worker expresses ignorance or error about a case or social welfare in general," and "Worker takes observer along on other stops unrelated to the job." Before I concluded that the idea for an index of trust was naive, the total number of variables had reached nineteen. Even though nearly every one of the nineteen variables was defined oppositionally, I didn't see this as a contradiction of the basic idea of an index.

The index was constructed on my tape-recorded field notes. Every two weeks I went through the list of workers and recorded my impressions of how I was getting along with each one. Unfortunately one worker, with whom I felt I shared a trusting relationship from the beginning, later revealed he had set me up during the first couple of weeks. He took me only to those safe welfare homes where nothing significant was happening. In addition to this, there were several other anomalies which more or less destroyed the plausibility of an index of trust. Eventually the notion atrophied, during the first couple of months, without much reflective thought. What did appear to make sense from these early experiences was that a relationship of trust was a *developmental process* to some extent *biographically specific* in nature. It appeared as an ongoing dialectic involving a multitude of cues, hints, signs, gestures, expressions, facial and body idioms, appearances, shared terminologies, commonly conceived living experiences, and so on. Of greater importance, these things are always subject to an ongoing subjective interpretation and reinterpretation, always changing in nature. It no longer seems plausible to think in terms of developing trust as a specifiable set of procedural operations. Rather, two or more persons engaged in a common course of social action may develop a sense of trust between them. It is a reality necessarily fluid and changing, always subject to reinterpretation. Given this understanding of the empirically unperceivable nature of trust, the following ethnographic materials will shed some light on the operations of developing trust.

PRACTICAL PROCEDURES USED FOR DEVELOPING TRUST

This section describes the strategies, ideas, practices, and procedures involved in the field-research situations at Metro. As an important prelude to understanding such matters, it should be pointed out that (1) some of these materials were culled from the study of how the members went about developing trust and how they talked of it, (2) the awareness of some of these phenomena results from some of the members' creative insights rather than just those of the observer, and (3) the strong overtones of instrumentality result from the practical necessities of doing a report such as this one. There is always more to the story than such glosses tell in so many words. On the other hand, this situation shouldn't obscure the issue of instrumentality altogether.

USING RECONSTRUCTIONS OF ONE'S BIOGRAPHY

In gaining entree to Metro, I had presented an idealized self. Later I realized this could result in some stigmatization, since clearance came from the administration. This realization, combined with some of my friends' observations that I was considered a hard person to know, suggested to me one of the initial strategies for fitting in, the strategy of identity spoilage. This strategy was effected to construct a front of humility, to appear as a humble person who would be a regular guy and do no one any dirt. This was done by using reconstructions of my personal biography. These reconstructions I typically presented by telling ironic tales on myself, by relating in the course of routine conversations various stories wherein the formal rationality of the ideal self was presented as crumbling under irrational exigencies of circumstances. Some involved situations that are thought to reflect common human foibles: commonly experienced situations known to be at variance with the idealized public morality or situations where the unanticipated consequences of my actions had rendered asunder the best-laid plans of the rational actor.[10]

It generally appeared to be the case that reconstructions of my personal biography utilized a procedural rule of minimizing social distance between the situated self presented in the reconstruction and the other person in the situation. Such a rule does not adequately account for all the variations in such reconstructions, however. This procedural rule was mitigated in actual use over time by the sex of the other party and the extent to which it was thought that a relationship of trust had developed. In a few instances, such reconstructions were used for other purposes.

In the early months of the research such biographical reconstructions were utilized within the context of a strategy of playing it safe which excluded matters of sex, ethics, and politics. For example, early in the research, when talking with one worker who had grown up on a farm, I used biographical reconstructions which related to my early boyhood on a farm. When talking with another worker who had grown up in a city, I used accounts reflecting my early boyhood in the city. In a conversation with one social worker, when she told about those portions of her biography relating to her difficulties with school, I reconstructed my biography similarly. When another worker talked about the relative ease with which he passed through school, similar reconstructions were presented from my experiences. In the early months, we could make use of these devices for managing each other's publicly presented morality. This transpired by means of the negotiation of ideas of shared experiences, thus making use of the common-sense procedural rules of identity and correspondence.

At first, the timing and appropriateness of the biographical reconstructions were judged by taking cues from others. Perceptions of these cues were often related to common-sense ideas about types of persons or understanding of the flow and tonus of the conversation in progress. For example, it was usually the case that male social workers talked relatively readily about matters of politics and sex, whereas female social workers periodically mentioned concerns with religion. The relationship was not at all dichotomous. In a situation as this, taking cues from others means that one makes use of the procedural rule of identity to determine the appropriateness of the intended reconstruction.

The contexts within which biographical reconstructions were used varied greatly. Not all contexts were either directly or indirectly relevant for any strategy of developing trust. After months of observations and after accompanying a given social worker on many visits to the homes of welfare clients, I saw that either or both of us would tire of the routine inquiries of social welfare. On some of these occasions we would use such biographical reconstructions as a device for transcending the here of our physical presence and the now of our immediate consciousness. By using the transcendental potential of language, we could use our biographies to attempt to draw a common delight from the immediate situation. Uses of biographical reconstructions were also occasioned in conversations called bull sessions by the members of the group. Such conversations are often consciously directed away from the immediacies of the here and now. They are attempts commonly understood to spice up the prevailing bureaucratization of spirit with some juicy stories of erotic experiences or tales of adventure. In situations as these, the procedural rules of relevance guiding accounts were not those for explicating some Archimedean notion of what really happened back then. Rather, the rules of relevance concerned fitting in, participating—in short, the meanings of membership. During one such conversation I reconstructed in rather colorful detail an experience in a Bangkok whorehouse even though I've never been to Bangkok. This experience has also been reconstructed on occasion by a former acquaintance of mine. Following one session, one of the members used the term "trading whoppers" to refer to these activities. It is questionable whether or not he intended these terms to cast doubt on their epistemological status. Unlike the following description about my putative political beliefs, the epistemological integrity of such accounts as the Bangkok whorehouse story is virtually assured by audience segregation from available discrepant information which could be used to invoke variations of the consistency rule.

The strategy of playing it safe just atrophied over time, at least in many cases. As subsequent materials document, there were some instances where the tolerant civility of playing it safe either was the only procedure used throughout the ten months to accommodate to the situation or waxed and waned with other procedures and other strategies. In most instances where relations involving a sense of trust were eventually developed, however, I subsequently used more and more intimate information in biographical reconstructions. This included information which expressed personal beliefs on matters such as politics, religion, sex, and contemporary events. Probably in the majority of these situations I was not aware of any conscious manipulation of the information. For the most part, the reconstructions seemed to come naturally, perhaps in the sense of Dr. Faustus' encounters with Mephistopheles.

However naturally such accounts did or did not come, it can be said with certainty that they came a little less naturally after one particular conversation. This occurred at the beginning of the eighth month at Metro. The conversation took place in the coffee room with a social worker who was one of my most trusted intimates at the time. While reflections cannot establish, nor do field notes indicate, whether or not there I ever stated my political beliefs unambiguously, I had made many comments which suggested I was, in matters of politics, a "radical–liberal." This was the term used by this intimate on many occasions to identify his own political stance. Now, during the conversation in question, he presented me with certain statements made to him by one of the other workers in the office. Taken on their face, they appeared to warrant an inference that I was in fact a conservative. Since there had been many conversations over the months between myself and this intimate, I interpreted the comments in the context of invoking the rule of consistency. In replying to these remarks, I used a procedure of synthesizing discrepant identities. I told the intimate I was trying to obtain the most objective and accurate information possible on the wide variety of activities and personal experiences of social workers in the office. I said the previous experiences over the months had led to the suspicion that, due to the common association of youth with liberal political beliefs, my inaccessibility to those who thought of themselves as conservatives could possibly constitute a biasing factor of the research. So I said I sometimes resorted to talking like a conservative to discover how such persons viewed social welfare or the world generally. Thus, in this conversation, the concept of the researcher's role was used as a more general category to synthesize information which, when seen in a different light, had presented the appearance of discrepancy.

It is easy to imagine such an event readily escalating to the status of a crisis in field research. But I retrospectively concluded that just the opposite occurred. While this is admittedly speculative, I suggest that the explanation of the synthesis actually enhanced my "rep" in my intimate's eyes. In another situation involving different circumstances a month later, he expressed his surprise that an "academic pussy" (a term he sometimes used, not meant pejoratively) such as myself could be so shrewd.

The occurrence of the situation described above led to my subsequent reflections on these activities. Prior to this, it had been so obvious that one of the features accounting for the orderly appearance of the setting was the segregation of the people within the office that I was not aware my biographical reconstructions were also constructed within such a context. Prior to the situation described above, there were not even any field notes recorded to document this feature of the setting. The phenomenon of synthesizing the discrepant identities described above also illustrates the reflexive and self-preservative nature of everyday practical reasoning. When confronted with a particular practical task at hand and information which is discrepant or contradictory in nature, the practical actor will reflexively preserve the foundations of his reasoning by making sense of the apparent anomalies in the accounts.

NORMALIZING SOCIAL RESEARCH

As the previous analysis of gaining entree to Metro noted, my arrival in the setting brought forth feelings of apprehension, suspicion, and paranoia. All the social workers had previous personal experiences with social research. All had participated in questionnaire situations, interviews, and other research activities at one time or another. But the appearance of a participant observer who would be looking over their shoulders for an extended period of time was not a normal or routine occurrence.

During the early months of the observations, and to a lesser extent throughout the remainder of the research, I used a variety of accounts to explain the purposes of the research. The intention behind these accounts was to take the putative definitions of the research from the realm of the unique, the threatening, the unusual, the unexpected, to the realm of the normal, the predictable, the routinely manageable. This procedure is termed *nor malizing social research*. In the context of informal conversation, usually when the social workers and I were out in the field together, I would communicate the general idea that I was a person with a sympathetic understanding of social welfare. I often said that my previous experiences had led me to understand that many things didn't work in the fashion presented by the official lines in the textbooks. I said that I would not be cramming my understandings into the formally rational criteria of science for the purposes of the field observations. The typical explanation involved a contrast conception. To contrast my purposes, I would construct and present what I termed administrative questions or questions of efficiency, saying that I intended to increase our understandings of the realities of social welfare.

In efforts to normalize social research, the society one seeks to observe, describe, and analyze is partially created by the observer. The efforts to normalize social research were intertwined on many occasions with the biographical reconstructions mentioned earlier. Subsequent reflections on these accounts suggest that many were formulated by using a "hot iron" strategy. This strategy is based on a common-sense understanding that people will tend to withhold final judgments on their first impressions of a neophyte in a particular setting, but may change their evaluations when additional information is received. As with the old saw "strike while the iron is hot," the field-research version also stresses taking advantage of the opportunities in a new situation. It involves provision of background information about the observer to the audience—giving it a background to be considered should any discrepant facts emerge later. In actual use, I was not aware of using such a procedure. It was taken for granted. Only after being in the setting for months, during which I observed other new arrivals and neophytes make their opening moves, did I realize that this strategy was commonly known, and in fact used as a matter of daily routine.

Two of the most important ways of normalizing social research are (1) to normalize perceived deviance, and (2) to instruct members of the observed groups in how to manage a social researcher. In the first respect, as the members gradually allowed me to enter some of the back regions of their world, observations were allowed of some of the purposes for which a social worker's "day in the field" stands as a gloss. At first, the workers presented accounts of activities which, if interpreted by using the formal schema of bureaucratic rules, could be seen as deviating from those rules. One situation involved a social worker who wanted to stop at a jewelry store to pick up a watch while in the field. His account of this event was presented in defensive terms. Another situation involved a female worker's defensive remarks about her intention to work through her lunch hour in order to quit at four o'clock that afternoon, an hour early. She wanted to go swimming with a friend. My transformation of the seemingly deviant to the presumptively normal was done by using some variation of one of two accounts, and in some situations both. The first involved statements that my wife, a social worker at an adoption agency, often did the same thing, whether she did or not. The second account involved statements that most college professors didn't put in a full day either. On occasion I also speculated that, were the truth known, it would be discovered that the eight-hour working day constituted one of the myths of the technological society. It was typically the case that such efforts to normalize perceived deviance were made only once or twice with a particular worker in the office. In the latter months of the field observations, I could spend entire afternoons with social workers lolling about in a Jacuzzi, drinking beer on the banks of a local reservoir, or partaking of the services of a local massage parlor. By the time I came to participate in such activities, my outsider status was not at issue; no normalizing efforts were required. An appropriate dramaturgical circumspection had been appropriately established in the ongoing performance.[11]

Procedures for instructing the members on how to manage a social researcher stemmed from experiences in the early weeks of the observations. In several situations, during a visit to the home of a welfare client, the client would focus her comments on me, not distinguishing between the social worker and the observer. This situation resulted from a variety of circumstances including some instances where I was introduced as another social worker, a new worker trying to learn the ropes. At worst, the result was embarrassment experienced by the social worker; at best, it was an emergent contingency requiring additional managerial efforts.

From these early experiences, a practical common-sense theory was developed about how such occasions could be avoided or their probability minimized. I related this to the social workers. I would tell them that it appeared that the physical location of furniture in nearly all the homes visited included at the minimum a couch and an adjacent chair. From earlier experiences, it seemed interaction would not focus on the researcher if he was positioned at either end of the couch–chair combination. So the social workers were instructed to "manage" me to one end or the other, out of the direct line of fire, to reduce the chances that my presence in the setting would disturb the ongoing interactions. This procedure also fostered the appearance that I had appropriate dramaturgical circumspection in relation to workers' everyday activities, that I actually cared about causing them as little interference as possible—which, in fact, was the truth; I did care about this.

In the case of the research observations at the welfare offices, a variety of symbolic procedures served to normalize social research. Given my purposes, I perceived such procedures as practical necessities. But the obvious issue raised by such operations is the potential biasing influence on one's research. To what extent do such procedures alter the interactions within the setting? What is the influence of the field researcher's partial complicity in creating the very situations he seemingly only observes? In these observations of social casework, the possibilities included alterations in the activities of the social worker, the welfare client, or clients, or both of them together. All these occurred at one time or another during the investigation.

To determine influence on the welfare clients, I asked, usually after a home visit, whether the social worker thought my presence had altered the setting in any fashion. This was a double-edged inquiry. The elicited response provided information not only about the possible alterations of the setting but also about the social worker's perception of the constitution of the normal setting in the particular case.

Alterations resulting from introduction of an observer were varied. During the first week of observations at Metro and after a home call to a welfare client whose case the worker had had for over two years, the worker remarked, "I've never seen Mrs. Kocker as nice and polite as she was today; maybe I should take you along with me on all of my home calls where the clients are hard to get along with." Several weeks later, after a home visit with another social worker, the worker commented that "something seemed strange" about the home call just completed. He wasn't exactly sure what it was. Several days later, after a phone conversation between this worker and the client, the worker reported the client had been very disturbed that a researcher had been brought to the home visit. That was why she hadn't behaved normally. Two other cases involved foster homes. In the first, so many home visits were made to the home of Mrs. Pouch during the research that when the social worker informed her I was leaving the office in a week or so, Mrs. Pouch said that "things wouldn't seem normal" if the worker visited without me. In the second, I had been to the home of Mrs. Wilkinson more often during the research observations than any social worker. I had been to her home on many occasions with one or the other of two social workers in the Child Welfare Services units who each had a child in placement there.

In the majority of these home visits, the worker reported few alterations in the client's behavior while I was present.

To ascertain whether my presence during a home visit changed the activities of the social worker was more difficult. It occasionally happened that a social worker, after a home visit, would say that she or he had done something differently. This could mean making statements to the client that she or he didn't normally make, or wouldn't have made without me there. But this wasn't typically the case. Insofar as the social workers would comment about a change, the comments would usually be made within the week following the home visit. In some instances comments were made weeks or even months later. In addition to noting these comments, I would try to cross-check for possible other sources of change in the social workers' behavior on home visits. I related the calls made with a given worker over time to other events, such as a falling out with a particular person or a policy change. Even with these efforts, however, there was still reason to believe my procedures in finding out the effect of my presence were less than foolproof. During an interview conducted with one worker at the conclusion of the field observations, she commented that she thought my presence had a restraining influence on her in talking about sexual matters with the clients. This observation had not been made before even though we made many home calls together.

In addition to instances where the workers voluntarily commented on their observations of the effect of my presence, information was obtained periodically through third parties. These included trusted intimates who told me what they heard others say when I was not in the office. One instance involved four women in a coffee klatsch. I was never accorded even the most provisional membership in this group, but one of the members periodically relayed some of the conversations in exchange for certain information I provided to her, information that she then took back to the other group members as part of her contribution to the daily fare. Several of these information reciprocities were developed during the course of the field observations.

Using the Concept of Interest To Develop Trust

The fundamental procedures of any field observations are those involving uses of the concept of interest to construct the appearance of being interested. It might be plausible to think that some of these procedures could be defined in terms of grammatical or syntactical rules, so that, for example, one would simply take for granted the common-sense meanings of a question or take for granted that a reply to a question was a straightforward answer. But it is just as true that constructions of the appearance of interest involve paralinguistic communications such as the bodily and other involvement idioms analyzed by Goffman.[12]

The most pervasive means by which one presents his involvement in the situation at hand is the disciplined management of personal appearance, including clean-shavenness, suitable clothes, and so on. It should be remembered, however, that early efforts to gain entree included a false start. In preparing for the first conference with the assistant director of the county Department of Public Welfare, I presumed the ordering of personal appearances in the setting would be relatively homogenous. On the basis of this presumption I proceeded to shave off my moustache, have my hair closely cut, and don an unpretentious uniform left over from my high school graduation. After a sneak preview of the setting before commencing the observations, however, I concluded that such a presentation of personal decor not only was uncalled for but could possibly generate a social distance between myself and the social workers.

Throughout the research a middle-of-the-road strategy was used in presenting my public self. In this respect, I avoided features those in the offices termed "conservative" and those they termed "way out." [13] To a degree, they perceived how one presented oneself publicly as related to formal policy statements of particular district offices, the personal preferences of a given administrative official, or "the way it's always been done around here." One of the social workers at Metro commented:

You can still be a hippie and work at Metro, but not a dirty hippie. There are some limits everywhere I guess, although I think they're as loose at Metro as they are anywhere else. Take [the] Mountain View [office], for example. If Fred would show up to work looking like that, I'm sure they'd kick him out before he walked in the door.

For the most part I presented facial and other bodily idioms in a given situation with a view to fostering the appearance of being involved or being interested in the actions of others. In many situations these idioms corresponded to the operations of my mind at the moment. In others they constituted a front for other activities, for example, thinking of the next question to ask or making note of a remark mentioned earlier in the conversation. To a surprising degree, the procedural rules for such operations were often defined in terms unique to the native speakers in the setting. The eleven social workers included one who used the term "legally blind" in referring to himself and one having a glass eye. Another used no side involvements during her conversations; that is, she looked another person straight in the eyes instead of using the more typical combination of main and side involvements. Another person coordinated his main and side involvements to complement the other speaker; he would look the other person in the eye when the other wasn't looking him in the eye, and vice versa.

The procedural rules for managing the facial and eye presentations of others were additional bits of the tacit knowledge used by the members to organize the setting. As mentioned previously, my procedures were developed only after a period of extended interaction with the members in the setting. In the beginning I used the common-sense cultural wisdom which indicates that newcomers to a setting are often exempted from some of the normative expectations. I felt my way around to discover features of the setting. In retrospect, it appears that the first months in the office were characterized by a studious presentation of face. But in later months, as more intimate relations with many of the members developed, I presented my face more in accord with a simultaneous imputation of motive to the speaker. For example, as a speaker's conversation developed, I might present a surprised, chagrined, hopeless, or humorous facial expression in accord with the judged intentions of the speaker as he relayed information. Also, over the course of time some individually specific interaction cues were developed with some of the members. These were used for connoting recognition of a joint understanding or an interpersonal relationship that had special status. For example, in catching the glance of one worker about to be approached by a supervisor commonly known as an unrelenting talker, I might roll my eyes and raise my eyebrows to communicate a commonly understood "Here we go again" message. On one occasion I took the reception of this cue to mean that I should walk over and interrupt the conversation. I did so, after which the intimate thanked me for having "saved me from a fate worse than death."

At least as important as direct presentations of facial and other involvement idioms were a variety of practical activities done to provide empirical foundations for a common-sense inference of interest. Such activities are called field-work reciprocities in the sociological literature.[14] During the course of the research investigations I served as a driver, reader, luggage porter, baby-sitter, moneylender, ticket taker at a local conference, notetaker, phone answerer when business was heavy, book reader, book lender, adviser on the purchase of used automobiles, manager of arrangements for going-away parties, bodyguard for a female worker assigned to investigate a situation where a woman was waving a gun around, letter writer, messenger, and other things. I attended meetings of many voluntary associations to which the workers belonged. I picked up one welfare client at six o'clock in the morning for transportation to the hospital so the social worker wouldn't have to get up so early. I played at various sports with the male workers. I helped one worker move to a new apartment. I helped with the arrangements of two funerals, canceled previous arrangements to spend an evening giving consolation to one intimate who discovered the man she loved had just been married, sent birthday presents, and so on. By engagement in activities such as these the appearance of interest was constructed. Perhaps the construction of such appearances leads to the phenomenon of "going native" in sociological and anthropological field work.

USING PLURAL PRONOUNS AND THE CONCEPT OF SOCIAL ROLE TO CONSTRUCT THE APPEARANCE OF MEMBERSHIP

Two of the commonly used devices to operationalize the principle of fitting in involve plural pronouns and the concept of social role. With regard to social role, I gradually became aware of the distinctions the members made with this concept. These distinctions were used similarly to present the appearance that I was "one of us," and not "one of them." In some conversations this apparent membership was communicated by using the substantive terminology, such as "social workers," "welfare clients," "supervisors," "administrators," and "switchboard operators." If the contextual referents of these roles were clearly defined and appropriate in a given conversation, the plural pronouns "us," "we," "they," and "them" were used.

As previous comments document, the efforts to construct the appearance of membership were problematic and variously successful. During the first couple of weeks at Metro, I accepted less-than-limbo-membership status as a field researcher's fate. I did not feel particularly unwanted because I had not been invited to so-and-so's party. However, at the end of the second month of field research at Metro, I learned of preparations for an all-office party to commemorate the departure of the assistant chief of the office. Even though none of the social workers had taken the initiative to extend a formal invitation to attend this affair, I thought that I had been around long enough to demonstrate my dramaturgical loyalty to the members. Also, knowing that none of those present would have any way of knowing I hadn't been invited, I took the initiative and extended an invitation to myself. In retrospect, it appears this party was my rite of passage. I was subsequently invited to attend such affairs by the members whenever they occurred.

USING PLURAL PRONOUNS TO CONSTRUCT
THE APPEARANCE OF POWER

Throughout the course of the field observations I tried to dodge any member's expectations that because I was a doctoral candidate in sociology, I was canonized with expertise in matters relating to social behavior. Professions of ignorance were typical when confronted with such matters, especially when I was asked to comment about a particular welfare case. There were several other instances, however, when I perceived that a profession of ignorance would foster the appearance that a Dagwood Bumstead had somehow stumbled into a doctoral program. Some situations seemed to call for the presentation of at least a cursory familiarity with social science knowledge. Such discussions were typically related to more abstract concerns than a particular case involving a welfare client. The presentations would often include the pronoun "we" to foster the appearance that the social science knowledge presented was powerfully shielded from an ontologically fatal insight about its actual subjective nature and possessed the powerful warrant of consensual validation.

This is not to say these conversations involved just so much rhetoric. In many situations, presentations of social science knowledge—whether by myself or others—were made within the context of discursive uses of the language. There were other occasions, however, where the powerful symbology of science was used rhetorically. The operational context distinguishing these usages on my part appears to have been, at least in retrospect, not so much a desire to impress others with expertise as a realization that others thought of such rhetoric as the only plausible or convincing language. In a few instances, the concept of profession was accorded a similar symbolic power. Several social workers had developed a notion of a professional self which they regarded as central to their conceptions of self. On several occasions, the pronoun "we" was used to similarly accord power to this notion, since I intended to leave the setting the same way it was upon my arrival insofar as this was possible.[15]

USING CHARM IN DEVELOPING TRUST

One of the methodological procedures mentioned by five of the thirteen social workers and two of the five inside informants, on independent occasions, was the use of charm. In most of these comments the term was used in reference to one of the bodily idioms presented throughout the research, my smile. On two occasions something such as "you are charming" was said, as if to remark on a feature of my substantial self.

Investigating the use of charm as a methodological procedure of sociological research was not one of the consuming passions of my work. However, since my colleagues over the last several years have not commented similarly, I am not inclined to think the meaning of this methodological procedure lies in the area, suggested by the word's etymology, of magic or occult power. It is more plausible to recognize the relevance of Aldous Huxley's remark that Lawrence's charm was that "he could never be bored." Not being subject to the same administrative sanctions as the social workers in the office, not being subject to the day-in and day-out work routines, the work schedules, the deadlines, the emergencies, the forms, the reports, the piles of rules and regulations and their continuous changes, the phenomenon of not being bored is the field researcher's luxury. No wonder a few found me charming on occasion. I was the fifth wheel on the bus; my bread was buttered elsewhere. In terms of keeping the ongoing routines ongoing, the affable, smiling field researcher is expendable.

The data and experiences are far too limited to examine charm in terms of the procedural rules of field research. The implication of mentioning it as included in the field researcher's repertoire is that its use represents a kind of plus in field research—specifically, that its use fosters the collection of more valid and reliable data in field research. But while there may be a grain of truth to such a claim in some isolated instances, the field experiences at Metro suggest that such a one-sided argument is oversimplified. It is worthy of note that during the same week when a supervisor at Metro commented it was pleasant to have my "charming smile" around the office, she was engaged in an attempt to have me removed from the setting.

SUMMARY AND CONCLUSIONS

This chapter began with the observation that all field researchers agree on the critical importance of personal relationships involving trust for gathering valid data in social research. This emphasis receives much attention in the traditional field-research literature. Also noted was the existence of four common-sense theories of developing trust that are found in the literature, each of which possesses a certain ring of truth. None of these common-sense theories stems from rigorous investigation of what social researchers actually do in real situations of human interaction. Rather, they all stem from the theorist's selective remembrances and reflections. While there appears to be a common consensus among the traditional field researchers that being honest, being open, and being a nice guy are in some manner related to the validity of data collected during a field investigation, further procedural specifications of what these actions consist of are not provided the reader. Furthermore, as was noted, the nature of these actions is commonsensically assumed to be motivationally impersonal and biographically transparent. In different terms, these are presumably the actions of Anyman.

By making the field research itself a topic for investigation, this chapter analyzes some of the taken-for-granted operations actually used in a number of real social research situations. These materials suggest that even though a field researcher chooses a setting for an investigation, in a fundamental sense he is thrown into a situation which exists in partial independence of his decisions and strategies. It is this sense of being thrown into the social world which Heidegger has analyzed as *Mitdasein,* or "being with others." Such a situation is, without hope of remedy, a very *personal* one for all those involved.

All social research is personal in three important ways. First, any investigation which involves the collection of data and the creative organization of data into a rational account of social order is, in the most fundamental sense, dependent on the investigator's intention to achieve just this. It is true that it is impossible to accomplish such an intention alone or as an individual. But without an intention to create a rational account of social order there would be no research findings as such. The available evidence shows that the origins of such motivating intentions are very diverse. There is even some evidence which suggests that oppositional value commitments can serve as an inspiration for scientific research.[16] Whatever their source or nature, however, these personal intentions are the basic ingredients of any investigation.[17]

Second, research enterprises are fundamentally personal in that they are seen to be so in a common-sense way by members of a particular social setting. Men of common sense do not typically make use of the ancient Greek distinction between knowledge and interest. Plato phrased it as the distinction between *logos* and *doxa,* and Weber revised it as one between facts and values. This distinction allegedly grounds a social scientist's claim to disinterested observation. Men of common sense view all knowledge as being use-oriented, as being related to the personal interests and practical purposes of the knower. They see a field researcher as someone who has an interest in his observations in the fundamental sense that he cares about them. They want to know not only what the investigator is up to but also whether or not he is a trustworthy person. In this respect, the observer's personal characteristics will be combined in a variety of ways to make imputations of motive, intention, and purpose and to evaluate moral character. Numerous putative traits such as one's sexual status, racial status, socioeconomic background, educational background, and personal biography may be used to make such determinations. Furthermore, these are combined with other common-sense cultural understandings about the observer's deference, demeanor, and presentation of himself as evaluations of moral character and trustworthiness are made. The traditional field-research literature may presuppose that a field-research enterprise is motivationally impersonal and biographically transparent, but these are not the assumptions of the common-sense actors in the setting.

The third way that research is personal relates to the operational procedures used to conduct a field project. As the materials presented in this chapter clearly show, *the methodological morality of field research is an accommodative morality.* To establish and develop relationships of trust for the purpose of obtaining valid observations, the operational procedures are guided by the principle of fitting in. This is to say that the investigator strives to maintain the integrity of the persons and situations encountered. The various operations described in this chapter such as the strategy of minimizing social distance, normalizing perceived deviance, the playing-it-safe and middle-of-the-road strategies, use of the concept of social role, and so on, may all be conceived as operations to maintain the integrity of the face-to-face situation at hand. Deciding how, when, and with whom to apply such operations in actual situations is beyond doubt specific to the persons involved as participants in these interactions. Furthermore, in several instances, only after engaging in a course of action over a series of weeks or months did I learn how it had been interpreted. In different terms, a decision that a certain course of action was correct in a situation sometimes followed the course of action actually taken in it and hence was made on the basis of retrospective interpretation. In this light, it is inappropriate to conceive of the strategies reported here as comparable to those commonly straightforwardly employed in games such as chess, cards, and sporting contests.

To refer to the procedures of field research in terms of a methodological morality is to suggest that all participants saw unambiguously clear meanings in interactional sequences and, furthermore, that these meanings were shared by those involved. And yet this chapter included some evidence that this is not always so. In one situation, a social worker presented me with what could plausibly be seen as discrepant information about me. This situation involved, on my part, a procedure of synthesizing discrepant identities. Certain mythical accounts were used to bridge this potential gap and to restore the equilibrium. And so the myth of the researcher's role and the myth of disinterested observation were maintained. Another situation involved my use of plural pronouns to construct the appearance of power. This represented another instance in which the moral meanings of a social phenomenon were not mutually shared by the participants in a face-to-face situation. In those situations where constructions of the appearance of power are used without any considerations of the moral meanings of things to the other parties, field research may be appropriately conceived as of a political nature. In this light, the *accommodative* morality of field research conceived here is to be distinguished from the absolutist morality of various radical modes of social inquiry which endeavor to subjugate the practical world of daily affairs to unambiguously defined rules. As analyzed by Egon Bittner, these radical modes of inquiry include religion, politics, and science.[18]

NOTES

1. Alfred Schutz, "Concept and Theory Formation in the Social Sciences," *Journal of Philosophy,* 51 (April 1954): 266–7.
2. Morris S. Schwartz and Charlotte G. Schwartz, "Problems in Participant Observation," *American Journal of Sociology,* 60 (January 1955): 344.
3. Howard S. Becker, "Problems of Inference and Proof in Participant Observation," *American Sociological Review,* 23 (December 1958): 652.
4. Rosalie H. Wax, "Reciprocity as a Field Technique," *Human Organization,* 11 (1952): 34–7.

5. John P. Dean, "Participant Observation and Interviewing," p. 233, in John T. Doby, ed., *Introduction to Social Research.* Harrisburg, Pa.: Stackpole, 1954.

6. Ned Polsky, *Hustlers, Beats & Others.* Chicago: Aldine, 1967: 133–4.

7. Chris Argyris, "Creating Effective Relationships in Organizations," *Human Organization,* 17 (1958): 34–40.

8. The project referred to here involved an investigation of an official course at Western University proposed as an experiment in "radical education." I, the observer, was formally the teaching assistant for the course, although such a formal designation became meaningless because of the "radical" nature of the experiment (and also because there was no teaching or grading to assist). As these events developed, the class members divided themselves into several factions, each of which was more or less impenetrable by those from other factions. The phrase "the problem of following the path of least resistance" refers to my failure to recognize that I had become socially defined as a member of one of the factions and hence was not able to participate with the members of the other groups on an equal footing. The research investigation was reported in an unpublished paper titled "Normalizing Social Revolution," 1970.

9. See Melville Dalton, *Men Who Manage,* New York: Wiley, 1959; Chris Argyris, "Diagnosing Defenses against the Outsider," *Journal of Social Issues,* 8 (1952): 24–34; and Robert L. Kahn and Floyd Mann, "Developing Research Partnerships," *Journal of Social Issues,* 8 (1952): 4–10.

10. It should be obvious that I owe an enduring intellectual debt to the scholarly analyses of Erving Goffman, who is at least indirectly responsible for inspiring many of my interests in the nature of everyday life through his writings. Those most relevant to these concerns are *The Presentation of Self in Everyday Life,* Garden City, N.Y.: Doubleday, 1959; *Behavior in Public Places,* New York: The Free Press, 1963; *Interaction Ritual,* Garden City, N.Y.: Doubleday, 1967; and *Relations in Public,* New York: Basic Books, 1972.

11. Goffman, *The Presentation of Self in Everyday Life,* pp. 212–16, 218–28.

12. Goffman, *Behavior in Public Places*.

13. Several field researchers have remarked that researchers are often accorded a kind of situational exemption from the normative conventions of a given group. In writing about the conduct of field research among adult criminals, for example, sociologist Ned Polsky has observed that they expect a researcher to act differently and that there are compelling practical reasons why the researcher should not "act like one of the boys." See his *Hustlers, Beats & Others*. William Whyte has even reported an instance where he was rebuked by the street-corner boys for adopting their ways of swearing. See his *Street Corner Society*. Chicago: The University of Chicago Press, 1943, 1955.

14. See Joseph R. Gusfield, "Field Work Reciprocities in Studying a Social Movement," *Human Organization*, 14 (1955): 29–34.

15. In an age when scholars of many different persuasions have questioned the distinction between the factual and the normative, the differences between a discursive and a rhetorical use of the language, and the self-fulfilling and self-denying prophetic meanings of verbal and written communications, it can only be stated that in trying to describe the actual practices of this research project, it is not my intention to promote some new strand of Quintillian dogma for the social sciences.

16. On the whole there are few personal accounts written by scientists elaborating their private motives or the feelings which have inspired their work. The most candid account in this respect is James D. Watson's account of the behind-the-scenes activities leading to the development of DNA. See his *The Double Helix*. New York: Signet, 1969. For a collection of reflections by sociologists, see Irving L. Horowitz, ed., *Sociological Self-Images*. Beverly Hills, Calif.: Sage, 1970. Another series of personal accounts and reflections on previous researches is contained in the various volumes of *Issues in Criminology*. To date these journal articles include interviews with James Short, Howard S. Becker, David Matza, Richard Quinney, Marvin Wolfgang, Daniel Glaser, and Anthony Platt.

17. In one sense this point might appear to be obvious, but in another sense it is not. The traditional field research literature contains a variety of accounts of the problem of "going native," referring to

the field researcher's immersion in the setting to the point that he actually *becomes a member* of the group he was supposedly studying. See Benjamin D. Paul, "Interviewing Techniques and Field Relationships," pp. 435 ff. in A. L. Kroeber et al. eds., *Anthropology Today: An Encyclopedia Inventory,* Chicago: The University of Chicago Press, 1953; Arthur J. Vidich, "Participant Observation and the Collection and Interpretation of Data," *American Journal of Sociology,* 60 (1955): 356–8; Colin M. Turnbull, *The Forest People,* London: Methuen, 1961, p. 209. For an article which addresses a related issue, see S. M. Miller, "The Participant Observer and 'Over-Rapport,' " *American Sociological Review,* 18 (February 1953): 97–9. In addition to these discussions of the problem of going native, it is also commonly known that there are a number of people who complete all the requirements for the Ph.D. degree except the dissertation, and there is even a special terminological designation for the phenomenon—"ABD," or "all but dissertation."

18. Egon Bittner, "Radicalism and the Organization of Radical Movements," *American Sociological Review,* 28 (1963): 928–40.

Chapter 5

Personal Relations and Data Collection

THE PREVIOUS CHAPTER began with the observation that the traditional field-research literature indicates consensus on the importance of establishing and maintaining personal relationships of trust in field research. This consensus presumably stems from the common-sense presumption that people may have things to hide from a researcher or, for myriad reasons, may make comments which are other than true. On the basis of this presumption, it is considered that developing relations of trust will eliminate any biasing influences or minimize their effects to the extent possible. Rather than a trivial matter of methodological technique, then, the development of personal relations of trust raises the crucially important moral issue of all social science research, the validity of the observations. Only a principled version of social science committed to the progressive elimination of such biases can appropriately claim to be a disciplined form of inquiry.[1]

In addition to the consensus on the importance of developing relations of trust, the previous chapter noted the existence in the traditional literature of four theories of developing trust in field

118

research. Each of these had a common-sense character, and the point was stressed that this was also true for the theory of developing trust put forth in Chapter 4. But let us put this issue aside for the moment. Let's assume, for the purposes of argument, that a field worker has established relations of trust in a research setting. Then what? The traditional literature is hazy on this point, but it is implied that two things occur at this juncture. First, the previously problematic entree situation changes with the development of trust. It becomes stabilized or at least is transformed into a kind of equilibrium where working agreements are shared. The researcher has explained the project and his good intentions and has demonstrated commitment to his statements in actual practice. Presumably the people in the setting no longer have grounds for distrusting the researcher. They will not keep any of the inside secrets from him, since relations of trust are now established. Second, the researcher is now able to collect valid observational data. To combine these two implications of the literature in different terms, developing trust is conceived in the literature as magically opening a door to collection of valid and reliable data. That this metaphorical door is seen to be magically opened is evidenced by some of the current articles on the phenomenon. For example, Richard Berk and Joseph Adams theorize on the nature of the mystery by arguing that "good participant observers . . . are born and not made." [2] The implications of such an argument for graduate training in sociology are truly radical in nature.

In all candor, I must say that prior to my social welfare investigations I expected that relations of trust would lead to, if not the magical opening of a door, something of a similar nature. This expectation was not the result of some wild speculation on my part. This was the impression gained from reviewing the traditional field-research literature in the social sciences. This was before the research experiences afforded me an understanding of John Lofland's observation that the traditional literature only reports "the second worst things that happened" [3]—that is, not the worst things.

The implied relations between developing trust and collecting valid data in participant-observation research, as described in the traditional writings, are so overformalized, ambiguous, and overrationalized as to constitute a distortion of what actually occurs in a research investigation. There are some exceptions to this general assertion. Certain qualifications are always necessary. But I believe the general truth of this statement is unassailable.[4] Much of the traditional field-research literature was written during a time when many sociologists were very concerned with making their endeavor a professional and respectable one. It was also a time when field researchers, occasionally called "soft-data people," were clearly on the defensive as they tried to justify their efforts in terms of the criteria of truth advanced by the positivistic objectivism model of science.[5] Given these facts, perhaps it is understandable why some of the anomalous features of scientific conduct were not publicly reported. While the historical and comparative works on the sociology of knowledge provide some useful understandings of science, they do not tell us what actually occurs in the conduct of science.

The research observations and experiences reported in this volume stress a more complicated picture of participant-observation inquiry than previously reported. Of primary importance in this respect are my research experiences, observations of the research process, reflections, and many talks with others, including many social workers and professional associates. Of secondary importance is one portion of the research itself. This involved observations of the *other* research projects conducted at Metro during the field investigation. These observations were not anticipated prior to the field research.

During the field investigations at the welfare agencies I witnessed bits and pieces of about a dozen other social research projects. One of these was a large research project being conducted by a private corporation, three were being conducted by persons from ancillary welfare–rehabilitative facilities as a condition for receiving their matching grants, one was a federally funded project distinct from such conditions, and the remainder were conducted by graduate students working on advanced degrees at local colleges or universities. This relatively large number of research projects probably resulted from the topical relevance of welfare concerns and welfare agencies' traditional cooperation with those with research interests. Observing the social workers cooperate with these other research projects served to stimulate my thinking about how individuals respond to social research situations.[6] I concluded that the responses people gave to a researcher's requests for information were related to several different sets of considerations. One set involved the practicalities of the response situation. These included the time available for the response, the amount of space provided on written forms, the temporal coordination of this activity with others, considerations of the existent status relations of the setting, a concern for minimizing the inconvenience of the other, and so forth. Another set of considerations involved the respondent's feelings at the moment. On several occasions, for example, right after social workers had completed an interview or questionnaire which was part of a research project, they would comment that their responses were related to how they were feeling at the moment. Another set of considerations involved the workers' putative judgments about how the research information would be used, by whom, for what purposes, etc. The major point of all these observations of other research projects is this: the considerations noted above do not give other research approaches faults which are necessarily remedied by using participant-observation research; these considerations are potentially applicable to all research approaches.

Personal relations of trust are the basic ingredient for a research project which intends the collection of truthful information, data which retain the integrity of the actor's perspective and social context. Such relations are essential for any project which seeks to penetrate the public fronts of our everyday lives. But even relations of trust do not set everything right. There are several reasons for this. Despite the good intentions of the researcher, efforts to befriend some members of the group being observed may not be successful. In those instances where elements of trust do exist, the meanings of the relationships may vary from individual to individual and may change over time. Efforts by the observer to befriend some individuals may antagonize others. Some actions by an observer may produce consequences which were not, and could not have been, anticipated prior to the actions.

In addition to these problems of the personal relations between an observer and the individuals he seeks to study, there are several others as well, and this chapter describes some of them as they were encountered during this investigation of social welfare activities. An understanding of these various problems is useful in itself. It gives us a better understanding of the complexities of social research. More importantly, however, it stresses the necessity of using one's sociological competencies to evaluate the influences of these phenomena on the observational data collected.

PROBLEMS OF MANAGING AN INSIDE DOPESTER

When I began my first week of field research at Metro, I was immediately confronted with an inside dopester. This is a person who expresses an interest in directing the substantive concerns of a research project. To put it differently, he is one with his own ideas about what the researcher should study. During the first week it was obvious to all that I was "green," ignorant of the daily routines, and uncertain where to go next. One of the CWS supervisors took me under his wing at this juncture. He invited me to his office for informal talks during the first days. In these conversations I told him what I could about the research. I said I had not yet developed well-articulated hypotheses to test. The supervisor responded with some research ideas of his own. He may have done this because of my expressions of uncertainty, or perhaps because of the lack of other conversational topics. I don't know for sure. His research ideas involved the production of statistical cross tabulations. He expressed an interest in relating a series of social and psychological variables among welfare clients to the categorical aid classifications used by the Welfare Department.

The supervisor was persistent about his ideas, but I would not say he was dogmatically insistent that I adopt them. Throughout our talks he always left me some room for discretion in my responses. As I reflected on these talks while at home in the evening, I was aware of the traditional accounts of the problems of the inside dopester reported by others. I devoted considerable thought to what course of action I should take. The conclusion to all this thought and reflection was that I just didn't know what to do. Since I also experienced feelings of anxiety during the first weeks, I think it is fair to say I was afraid of doing anything at all. As subsequent events unraveled, I developed no plans or strategies; I took no self-conscious actions to manage the inside dopester. When the time to make a decision arrived, I acquiesced to the supervisor's requests. I informed him I would begin to investigate the ideas he presented to me.

During the first several weeks of the research, I read several books recommended by the supervisor. I took home several statistical forms for further study. Also, while at home in the evening I prepared comments and questions for my next talks with him. I tried to foster the appearance that I was hard at work on the aforementioned problems.

At the end of the fifth week of the field research, the supervisor left the office for a lengthy visit to Japan. He was gone for over six weeks. When he returned, he never mentioned his initial research interests again during the following seven months of the field observations. My subsequent relations with him were as good as those with most of the social workers, and better than those with many. I concluded the problem of the inside dopester had solved itself independently of any self-conscious actions on my part. Since the supervisor never mentioned his ideas after his return from Japan, I speculated that his initial research proposals were a kind of opening move on his part—a way to break the ice with a stranger, a way of feeling me out to see what kind of person I was. This was his way of obtaining information about me so that he could make reports to his workers at the time when the feelings of apprehension about the stranger were at their highest.

Problems of Relating to Freeze-Outs

Chapter 3 noted that after the first joint meeting with the two CWS units where the crucifixion occurred, I made the rounds in the office, gradually scheduling my days with each of the social workers. This procedure provided an opportunity to normalize their apprehensions and explain the purposes of the research project. Also, I didn't know of anything else to do. During these efforts, some workers began providing information about others' thoughts and feelings on the researcher's arrival. I discovered I was confronted with two "freeze-outs" among the thirteen CWS personnel. A freeze-out is an individual who expresses an unwillingness to aid the research. In one case the social worker informed me of this unwillingness and the reasons for it in a face-to-face conversation. In the other, the reasons were relayed to me through a third party.

When I talked with the first freeze-out, he said his recent arrest during the intradepartmental struggle with the Probation Department over the appropriate jurisdiction of runaway cases had made him "a little paranoid" lately. He additionally expressed his uncertainty about my trustworthiness. He concluded this talk by saying he thought the best policy in this situation was to "play it safe." He wanted to avoid taking unnecessary chances, especially since his legal case was pending. He told me that his decision was based on his particular personal situation and that he would not take action to proselytize the other workers about this. In my response to these remarks I used the notion of shared agreement and invoked an exception rule. I said I thought his judgments were thoroughly reasonable and furthermore, since the research project didn't involve any ideas of sampling all workers, his judgments would not impose any hardship on the research.

My relations with this worker underwent many changes. For the first few months our relationship was cordial but cool. There was no apparent change. While at home in the evening I occasionally prepared questions to ask him the next day. This was a strategic way to appear interested in his work activities. At the same time it fostered the impression that I held no grudges about his refusal to aid the research. During the third month of the research, without any indications the initial understandings had changed, he took the initiative to ask me to go with him on an investigation. It involved a community complaint of alleged child neglect. This kind of situation was often experienced as one of the more problematic for the CWS intake workers. I interpreted this request at the time as a signal that our relationship was improving, or at least as an indication that he was not influencing my attempts to develop relations of trust with the others.

During the sixth month of the research, however, what relationship there was began to deteriorate. To some extent, as I learned from others, the deterioration reflected the worker's changing evaluation of the wisdom of tolerating the presence of a social researcher. This was related to his assessment of the potential impact of the governor's proposed welfare reforms. His evaluation changed to the extent that he began presenting arguments to others about why it would be best to avoid befriending the resident researcher. My initial response to this was to do nothing. I felt confident that his arguments would have a relatively meager reception. I decided to accept the conflict as a field researcher's fate in a setting of pluralistic realities. After a couple of weeks, however, and some agonizing on my part, I changed my mind. I began to think there were prospective dangers in being a nice guy while a detractor was at work undermining the enterprise. I decided to join the fray. I formulated a strategy of undercutting to neutralize the effects of the detractor's arguments. This strategy consisted of verbal accounts which transformed his arguments into irony—that is, comments to others that his perceptions should not be taken at face value. The decision to take this action was partially a result of conferring with others in the setting about what I should do.

During these events the social worker enlisted the support of another CWS worker, a female friend of his. The two of them constructed several team performances to express their feelings about my presence in the setting. On one occasion, for example, the man dropped a large piece of cellophane over his desk chair so I wouldn't be tempted to sit at his desk. The paradoxical nature of such actions was that each member of the pair continued to be very friendly toward me as long as the other was not present. The relations with both remained touch-and-go throughout this crisis period of the research.

Within several weeks, things changed again. For no apparent reason, the first freeze-out began to trust me more and more. He eventually invited me to his home for private social affairs. During a conversation with one of the inside informants six months later, two months after the completion of the full-time observations at Metro, he said, "Having J.J. around was one of the best things that happened all year. He made me feel like I knew a lot about social work."

My relations with the second freeze-out were more problematic. During the first weeks of the field research, I noted that this worker wasn't at her desk when I was in the office. But as I was unfamiliar with the everyday routines of the workers, I saw no reason to think this was unusual. After nearly four weeks, one of this worker's close friends informed me she was "horrified" by my presence. Her daily actions had changed noticeably since my arrival, my informant said. She was engaged in extraordinary efforts to avoid contact with me. When I learned this, I felt chagrined because my presence had affected someone like this.

At first I thought it might be better for all concerned to utilize an avoidance strategy. I initially planned to avoid asking if I could accompany her on home visits to see welfare clients. I thought this would reduce her feelings of "horror." Then, after well over a month of the research period, I learned she was being subjected to importunity, teasing, and cajolery from her colleagues. My previous feelings of chagrin turned to guilt and shame. I also developed an irrational fear of meeting this worker face to face. During the eighth week of the research another one of her friends came to me. She said the situation in the coffee klatsch, where the teasing and cajolery were intense, had become unbearable. She asked if I would request to go with her friend on some of her calls. She said this would probably break the ice and get the situation over with. As I mustered the courage for the request during the next couple of days, two other workers in the office made the same request of me. The time had arrived to transcend irrational fears. As one might expect, the moment of the request was very different from what I had imagined in my private thoughts; it was worse. The freeze-out was exceptionally angry. She called me "sonofabitch" and said she would consent to my accompaniment on a home call only because she was under great pressure from her supervisor and colleagues to do so. Personally, she said, she didn't think too kindly about the whole idea. She said the selected home call would be "a set-up from beginning to end," and it was; the conversational protocol was prearranged by her in a phone conversation with the client. The methodical procedures of my response have escaped memory, but somehow we managed to pull it off together. The teasing and cajolery ceased.

The set-up home visit with the second freeze-out was the only one I made with this worker in ten months at Metro. One reason for this was my irrational fear of her. In the case of the first freeze-out, I accompanied him on only about ten home visits. This compares to approximately 150 home visits with another worker. Whatever the causes of these events, it must be said they affected the representability of the observations, although it is impossible to determine the extent in any absolute sense.

Observations of how the two freeze-outs conducted social casework were limited. But it was possible to learn about their activities from trusted intimates. My intimates' shared observations provide several clues about freeze-outs in sociological field research. Concerning the first freeze-out, his colleagues reported he had been "tightening his belt" and "playing it safe" for some time before my arrival in the setting. It was common knowledge that he used his days in the field as a front for a variety of other activities, the most important of which was job hunting. His case load was largely padded, meaning that he kept several case folders for clients for whom no services were provided. Several months later, he gave up even this pretense. I was able to verify independently that he had no official cases then; for reporting purposes he fabricated the entries on the forms. He had terminated all his official cases while maintaining the appearance he possessed a full case load.

Concerning the second freeze-out, her intimate friends reported that her case load was also largely padded. She padded it with inactive cases which could have been terminated by another interpretation of formal agency rules than the one she made so that she wouldn't receive any new cases. In the office this was not a secret. She openly acknowledged this was precisely what she had been doing for many months, even in front of the Metro chief and assistant chief. Her colleagues said she had been protected or covered in these actions largely because of a mother–daughter relationship with her supervisor. This had developed over many years. The supervisor referred to her as "my foster daughter" publicly. On several occasions the worker remarked about the protection her relationship afforded her. She once noted she had come a long way since that time, several years ago, when one of the welfare investigators found her asleep at home in the middle of the day.

The purpose of reporting these observations is not to point out inefficiencies of public welfare; actions very similar to these could be found in many settings—certainly at most universities, for example. Rather, they point to one of the limitations of the field observations. The actions called padding a case load were not confined to the two freeze-outs, and I was not completely restricted from observing instances identified as padding. On the whole, however, the field observations include only very little of this everyday welfare activity. Along with several other actions to be reported later, these led me to conclude that the field research possessed a *public-morality bias,* meaning the observations did not include welfare activities intentionally used for thoroughly private purposes. This will be discussed later.

Problems of Being Manipulated

Earlier remarks note that the research transpired during a period of turmoil. Some of the features of this included the recent arrests of social workers, the struggles between the local Social Services Union and the welfare administration, and the proposed welfare reforms. These events stirred great controversies. As far as the field research at Metro was concerned, however, there was another conflict more basic to the daily CWS activities. This was the conflict and competition between the two CWS units. This conflict had a long history. It had waxed and waned for over six years. It generally emerged only in the context of some other issue, rarely by itself, and did not engage the same commitments of all the individual social workers. To give an example of the strength of the feelings involved, during the final month of my field observations relations between the two units had deteriorated to the point where the assistant chief at Metro decided to physically separate them.[7]

In each CWS unit there were several workers who had begun their employment at Metro in one unit, had received below-standard personnel evaluations from their first supervisor, and had been transferred to the other unit. The supervisor of one unit was known as "the hatchet man of Metro." His unit was reputed to be the one where persons from other parts of the office were transferred when their supervisors desired to build a case for having them dismissed from CWS. The personnel-transfer procedure was called axing.

One instance of the intraunit struggle involved a blind social worker and his previous supervisor. This worker began at Metro after finishing graduate school. He received a below-standard evaluation at the end of his six-month probationary period, was axed, and was sent to the other unit (the one supervised by the hatchet man). Even though he had been in the second unit for six months before I arrived on the scene, it was commonly known that his former supervisor was still out to get him. She didn't feel blind persons should handle CWS case loads. She had taken various actions trying to build a case against him, to justify his dismissal from CWS.

Five weeks after the research began, as noted previously, one of the supervisors left for a six-week absence. This left the remaining supervisor, who was the blind man's former supervisor, in charge of administering both units. Several days after her colleague's departure, she asked me to confer with her in her office. During this talk she tried to solicit my aid in her attempts to build a case against the blind social worker. Among other things she asked that I make available the field notes for my home visits with the blind worker. She was using the practical method of information getting and control that office workers commonly call backstabbing or going behind someone's back.

In contrast to my uncertainties about what to do about the inside dopester, I was thoroughly prepared for this contingency. I had devoted considerable thought to how such a contingency would be met if or when it occurred. My response to her requests could be called, I think, a strategy of obscurantism. This involved providing a rhetorical smoke screen. I elucidated numerous compelling reasons why a person with such arcane theoretical interests as myself was obviously unqualified to proffer observations about a worker's competency. I constructed a long account of the distinctive differences between the kinds of questions of interest to sociologists and those of interest to managerial personnel. My intentions were to provide a great amount of talk from which my cooperation with her efforts could be inferred and simultaneously to fail to provide her with any useful information. In most situations involving my usage of rhetoric, just how I was using it was beyond the ken of my awareness. This conversation, however, was one situation when the conditions for the classical notion of clear persuasive intent were met.

In reflecting on this conference, I think this is what occurred. The supervisor stated her purposes openly at the start of the conversation, apparently thinking that since I had been around the office for over a month, I would also consider it obvious the blind worker was incompetent. When, after thirty minutes, my comments failed to provide any documentation for this to her obvious fact, she recanted some of her opening remarks. She concluded our talk by saying that she had just been interested in learning how Jeff, the blind worker, was getting along. She did manage to put together a case against him, which she presented to the other supervisor on his return, but it was quashed without fanfare. The case did not, incidently, include any remarks from our conversation.

There were other attempts by some of the members to use me for their purposes at hand, but they were relatively minor and benign by comparison. None were as straightforward as that described above. I think the comments I offered during the talk with the supervisor were of such a nature that, if I may be speculative, she concluded I wasn't smart enough or observant enough to provide the information she sought.

The Problematics and Limitations of Trust

For over six months at Metro I had presumed that whatever trust was, eventually it would be possible to apprehend its basic character and develop it. Throughout this period, however, it had been obvious that my personal relations with the social workers were different and variable. This fact did not seem to be a falsification of my presumptions, only a limitation of them. I assumed that the reasons why relations of trust had not developed in particular instances were to be found in my procedures for demonstrating trustworthiness to the members. My presumptions began to change when I grasped what was, in retrospect, an equally obvious truth: the agency members experienced their relations *with one another* problematically. Once this was articulated, it continually surprised me that I had spent over six months believing in my presumptions about trust. They were invalidated on prima facie grounds every day, yet I had failed to turn this truth back on them.

This is not to say that in general the members at Metro *distrusted* one another. There were some instances of this, but for the most part individuals trusted some more than others, trusted some not at all, and often trusted some for some purposes but not for others. During my first six months I witnessed friendships and romances created and dissolved, and committees in every stage from originating idea to dissolution or atrophy. There were alliances, coalitions, and interoffice political factions. They were put together for the purposes at hand and dissolved when victories or defeats were consummated. And yet throughout these observations I thought I would be developing relations of trust in such a fashion that, at a magic moment, it would be possible to know these phenomena independently of the daily flux. I additionally assumed that at this magic moment what is called the problem of going native in the field-research literature would emerge as another, but different, problematic.

I would have to say in candor that I always knew people experience their relations with one another problematically. It isn't necessary to conduct field research to learn that. The essence of my seventh-month insight—the sort of revelation that other field researchers have termed an "ah-ha experience"—was the realization that I had failed to translate this common understanding into my thinking about the methods of social research. As soon as I did, an entire range of new problems emerged for further study. Ernst Cassirer has observed similarly:

> And so it remains true, even in highly developed knowledge, that each newly acquired concept is an attempt, a beginning, a problem; its value lies not in its copying of definite objects, but in its opening up of an entire problem complex. Thus while among the basic logical functions the judgment closes and concludes, the concept, by contrast, has essentially the function of opening up. In this sense a concept can be effective and fruitful for knowledge long before it is itself exactly defined.[8]

Prior to applying the obvious truth noted above to the research setting, I assumed that at some point in the inquiry I would try to delineate procedural rules for developing the trust of various types of informants in terms of the kind and quality of data collected. The idea that this is what one does is implicit in many of the traditional field-research writings. It is explicit in some.[9] It appears to be a reasonable inference to draw from the seemingly uncommonsensical writings of Erving Goffman that all one has to do to develop trust is penetrate the front regions of a setting or in some manner get behind the daily appearances of things.[10] From the research experiences reported here, it is clear the problems aren't this simple. This is especially evident in instances of inside dopesters, freeze-outs, and attempted manipulations of the observer.

Even in those instances where a sense of trust developed between myself and the social workers, the relations were more fluid, emergent, and situational than any definitive set of procedural rules could possibly articulate. At the most mundane level, individuals had bad days, or sometimes only bad mornings or bad afternoons. These were slices of experiential time when individuals not only didn't want to talk to the affable researcher but didn't want to talk to others in the setting either. The cues for recognizing such moments were typically individually specific. They included furrowed brows, blank stares, sharp or curt methods of talking, and so forth. Such cues constituted important bits of tacit knowledge used by the members to organize the setting. Often they would pick up on the cues as indices of the way an individual was feeling that day. An example is a comment like "Looks like that first call got Bill off on the wrong foot today. He'll be testy for the rest of the day."

Some daily variations related to how individuals were feeling. Others had to do with situations occurring earlier, like having a flat tire on the way to work, running out of gas, or being confronted with a crisis before having an eye-opening cup of coffee. Other variations resulted from events from one's private life, like discovering that one's fiancé had been wed over the weekend or that one's house had been burglarized. Eventually I termed these kinds of occurrences the *mini-dialectic* of personal relations in field research. I concluded it was impossible to elaborate an absolute set of procedural rules for learning about such occurrences. The important criteria for recognizing these features were situational. Even if possible to elaborate, however, the rules would be of dubious utility for methodological purposes.

The *maxi-dialectic* of personal relations in field research is more important methodologically, but it is equally difficult to describe these relations. Earlier materials described the changing nature of my personal relations with some of the CWS workers, including the inside dopester, the freeze-outs, the manipulative supervisor, and others. There were other changes too. Several of these will be briefly illustrated.

I was in the process of establishing relations of trust with one social worker, or so I thought, when all of a sudden the bottom fell out of our relationship. A close friend of his later reported the worker was "put off" because he thought I was winning the favor of an attractive woman who had previously rebuffed his advances. The woman was actually one of the inside informants of the research, a close friend of my wife. The CWS worker did not know this at the time, however.

There were several situations where actions taken to befriend one worker incurred the antagonism of others. In the case of the supervisor who tried unsuccessfully to have the research terminated during the tenth month, the most common explanation put forth by the other workers was that I had befriended the blind social worker. In a similar situation, my befriending of one worker became redefined as possible complicity by others opposing him in an interoffice political struggle. In another situation my methodology inspired the moral indignation of an older woman. To establish trust with one of the male workers, I had used a procedure known as throwing a roaring drunk, at a few infamous brothels of a neighboring community. In the subsequent storytelling the woman remarked to a friend that she thought I would have been ''above'' doing the kinds of things Frank was known to do. Little did she know.

These illustrations emphasize two major points about the conduct of field research. First, in any complex social setting the personal relations between an observer and the individuals he studies will emerge gradually and will be problematic. The personal relations are subject to changes, and it is incumbent on the investigator to assess the influences of these changes. Second, the complicated personal relations involved in a field-research project will necessarily create patterns in the field observations. To say this, however, is not necessarily to say the research is less objective. For example, the development of relations of trust constitutes a pattern which could actually result in more objective observations.

There appear to be several distinctive relations between the patterns of my observations and the patterns' effects. In some cases, independent evidence warrants judgment either that a given pattern is irrelevant to questions about the intersubjectivity of the observations or that the influence is miniscule. In other cases, independent evidence warrants a judgment that the objectivity of the research has been affected. For most of the patterns existent in my field observations, however, a fundamental uncertainty remains about their influences, if any. There are two important implications of this. The first is that it is impossible to rationalize social science knowledge in any absolute sense; when all is said and done, an element of mystery remains. The second important implication concerns the relations of the field observations, records, notes, and analyses to what gets reported as the research findings. This is the topic of Chapter 7.

The following materials will briefly depict the possible relations which may exist between the patterns of my research observations and their effects. I will describe, first, one pattern and note the reasons why it was judged irrelevant to the issue of the objectivity of the project. Then other patterns will be noted, and the reasons why they were considered as affecting the observations. These illustrations show that there are fundamental limitations of field-research observations even in those instances where relations of trust are developed.

In an interview conducted during the final week of the observations at Metro, I asked one female CWS worker if she thought my sex made a difference in her actions throughout the research. I asked if she thought she might have done anything differently if I had been a woman. She said my being male did make a difference. Then she paused momentarily, gave the question more thought, and said she wasn't certain what the difference was. She advanced the supposition that she engaged in more "woman-talk" when in the company of other women. She observed that she had done less of this on those days we had been together. I then recalled her earlier observation about a home call where she felt restrained in discussing the client's sex life. I asked if she thought this situation would have been different with a woman researcher along. She replied that it was hard to say for sure, but it might not have made any difference. She said the crucial factor was just having another person along with her; it might have been the same even if the other person had been a woman. She concluded this portion of the interview by saying she could not make a definitive judgment about this.

In retrospect, I've developed a sense that the ambiguous differences hinted at by this social worker are indeed real ones.

With an admittedly limited understanding of "woman-talk," however, my conclusion is that the kind of information one gets from engaging in it is not directly related to the knowledge I sought during the research. My conclusions support one of S. M. Miller's observations; on many occasions I was availed of more information than I needed to have, and on many others more information than I expected or wanted to have.[11]

Another pattern of the observations was also judged irrelevant for the research. It involved the workers' geographical selection of the home visits to which they would take me. Often, when the workers wanted to make a visit to a home in one of the out-lying areas, they went there directly from home in the morning to reduce driving time. They often made calls on the way home in the evening for the same reason. This meant there were several cases in each worker's case load I never observed. But since the worker's homes were spread out over an equal area, I concluded there was no basis for thinking that the research included any kind of geographical bias.

Independently obtained evidence suggests that other observational patterns produced what could be accurately termed a bias in the research. In one pattern, for example, I was systematically excluded from observing situations when the CWS workers had planned in advance to use what they defined as procedures for sanctioning welfare clients.[12] The three most commonly used expressions for these procedures were "coming on strong," "leaning on a client," and "pulling the rug out" (from under a client). This pattern applies mainly to the observations at Metro. Here the CWS workers were dealing with nonadjudicated cases. They were not formally deputized by the county. In three of the other offices the CWS workers were deputized, albeit with more limited mandates than police or probation officers. Here the workers dealt with adjudicated cases only. And these workers did not engage in the same efforts to keep the researcher from observing their coming-on-strong activities. On several occasions a worker from one of the latter three offices allowed me to witness such actions on the very first visit.

As early as the tenth week of the research at Metro I became aware of the possibility of such a bias. As I returned from a home visit one day, I met another worker in the parking lot. He called me aside and said he had something to tell me. He related comments of two other workers he had overheard in the office that morning. These two workers agreed they wouldn't be taking "the charming field researcher" to see certain kinds of situations. My intimate added that since he and I were close, he wanted to explain this to me. He told me I should not interpret this as an indication of any personal animosity. He informed me that with certain welfare cases it was sometimes necessary to come on strong—"to lean on them a bit"—to motivate the clients to take actions which would benefit them in the long run. He remarked, "Sometimes these things get a little messy." It wouldn't be reasonable to expect many workers to take me along on these occasions. He said it could be that none of them would ever do so.

During this conversation, as I remember it, I agreed with his judgment that this was reasonable, but I really didn't think his suppositions would prove correct. If his observations about what would happen to me in this regard were correct at the time, I thought, the others' apprehensions would disappear over time, after I had more opportunity to demonstrate my general trustworthiness.

The truth of my intimate's observations was established persuasively over the next eight months. Several of those with whom I later established relations of trust subsequently made similar observations. During an interview conducted in the final week of the field observations, one worker remarked that she liked me very much personally, thought I was pleasant and personable, and said she hated to see the field research concluded. She said she had thoroughly enjoyed the days we had spent together, a feeling which was mutual. She then went on to say that she had not taken me to see any situations where she thought it necessary to "pull the rug out" from under a client. She added that there were other situations too. These included several intimate friendships she had developed with clients over the years. She remarked that she kept some of these cases "on reserve," meaning that they afforded her a place to go when she wasn't feeling too well or didn't feel like discussing anyone's private troubles.

Why did this systematic exclusion occur? I concluded there were two major reasons. The first is relatively obvious. Such exclusion results from the irremediable paradox of mixing the metaphorical language of scientifically objective social case-work, a dubious result of decades of attempts to transform political and moral problems into managerial ones, with oppositional metaphors like "coming on strong," clearly suggestive of uses of power independent of moral or ethical considerations. But this isn't the whole truth of the matter.

The second major reason for the systematic exclusion is that the realization of one's intention to come on strong in a given instance is thoroughly problematic. I was able to observe several situations where the worker's intentions before the home call were altered drastically. Several went in like lions but came out like lambs. From my limited observations and many discussions with social workers about this, I concluded the problematic nature of the sanctioning practices was equally as important a reason why the social workers systematically excluded me from observing these events.

While the firsthand field observations of the preplanned sanctioning practices were few, I was able to learn about these actions. As soon as I realized the limitation of the field observations, I invoked a strategy of second-guessing. This was utilized during several of the many coffee-room conversations in which I participated. It was intended to elicit accounts of the sanctioning practices, to draw the workers out. To do this, I constructed fictitious accounts of sanctioning events which I claimed to have witnessed recently. I would then solicit the worker's evaluations of the typicality or familiarity of the account. This was a practical method for eliciting the worker's observations and reflections. A typical response to my fictitious account involved a worker in relaying the details of one of his or her casework experiences. I also used this method for drawing out the social workers' knowledge on other occasions. I did not, however, consider these accounts as appropriate substitutes for actual observations.

One might be tempted to consider some of the illustrations in this chapter as interesting field-research anecdotes. But they raise important theoretical and methodological questions. If relations of trust in a field-research project are indeed problematic and if the problematics entail limitations of the research observations, an assessment of these facts as they affect the validity of the observational findings is called for. With respect to the validity of my observations of social welfare activities, one conclusion to be drawn is that my systematic exclusion from situations involving the use of sanctioning procedures introduced a certain *routinization bias* into the research.[13] Since this bias involves features of the setting which were *not* observed, there remains a fundamental uncertainty in attempts to assess the exact nature of it. With respect to the situations where workers padded their case loads or held cases in reserve, there are similar grounds warranting a conclusion that the observations include a *public-morality bias*. As stated earlier, this means the observations do not include welfare activities intentionally used for thoroughly private purposes. One intimate informed me privately, for example, that from time to time he "had some things going for him" in his case load. This was a reference to sexual liaisons between him and his clients. He never, of course, took me along to witness these occasional realities of public welfare. On several occasions intimates described how and under what conditions formal rules and regulations of the agency could be, and were, manipulated for personal financial gain. On no occasion did I actually witness this, though. There is a lesson to be learned from these illustrations: even if a sociological field researcher feels confident that he has given his all to develop personal relations of trust in order to obtain valid intersubjective observational data, this does not set everything right. It is still necessary to assess the influences of the relations on the research data.

CONCLUDING REMARKS

The relevance of the materials presented in this chapter for our understanding of the conduct of field research is clear. The materials emphasize the crucial importance of developing personal relations of trust with the members in the setting where the investigation is conducted. This is essential for making the observer able to understand the interactional contexts of communications so that the knowledge generated by the project will be objective, or intrasubjective. But the materials in this chapter also show that even in those relationships where a sense of trust has developed between the observer and the individuals, this is not in and of itself sufficient to give the observer access to certain kinds of information and actions. Developing trust is a necessary condition for valid observations but not a sufficient one; it doesn't open magic doors.

This chapter supports several conclusions about personal relations in field research. First, the idea implicitly advanced in much of the traditional literature that a field researcher establishes trust with the members of a setting *as such* is a myth. Near the end of the welfare investigations I finally concluded that it is not a realistic possibility to develop relations of trust as such. This was especially true in a setting that included a radical leftist, a militant women's liberationist, older people, younger people, mods and squares, Republicans, Democrats, third-party members, Navy chiefs and commanders, Reserve Army majors, pacificists, conscientious objectors, and so on. Actually, the meanings of trust are individually and situationally specific. It is a practical necessity for a field researcher to make use of his common-sense knowledge and cultural wisdom about such persons and their interactional situations to assess the validity of the ongoing observations. The materials presented here also indicate that the relevant personal and interactional cues are typically defined contextually rather than structurally or syntactically. During the final months of the field research I gradually developed a notion of "sufficient trust" to replace the earlier presuppositions gained from a reading of the traditional literature. Sufficient trust involves a personal, common-sense judgment about what is accomplishable with a given person. For example, there is a realistic limit to what a fiftyish mother of four will tell a twenty-nine-year-old outsider who is a Ph.D. candidate at the local university.

Second, several of the illustrations in this chapter show that even when trusting relations exist, it is still necessary for the observer to record the observations with a keen sense of human beings' ongoing interpretations of past, present, and future events. It is always important to keep in mind the natural properties of the human knowing mind; for instance, sometimes things are forgotten.

Third, this chapter stresses the necessity of using one's sociological competencies to evaluate the observational data. Such evaluations are inevitably defined contextually rather than procedurally. The chapter notes instances where independent evidence exists to make a relatively clear evaluation and other instances where a fundamental uncertainty remains.

Finally, illustrations provided in this chapter suggest the existence of an irreducible difference of interest between an observer and the individuals he studies. This does not necessarily mean conflicting interest. To observe sociologically means that the observer deliberately cedes the social realities of the observations as not being *his* reality. The facts of life for the practical actors in the setting are, for the observer, exhibits for observation, recording, reflection, theoretical speculation, and so forth. The meaningful properties seen by the observer in the things observed cannot possibly be equivalent to the observed individuals' experiences of them. We shall return to this issue later.

NOTES

1. The phrase "principled version" is taken from Harold Garfinkel's discussion of the distinction between common-sense and scientific rationality. See his "The Rational Properties of Scientific and Common Sense Activities," *Behavioral Science,* 5 (1960): 72–83.

2. Richard A. Berk and Joseph M. Adams, "Establishing Rapport with Deviant Groups," *Social Problems,* 18 (1970): 108.

3. John Lofland, *Analyzing Social Settings.* Belmont, Calif.: Wadsworth, 1971, p. 132.

4. This observation is also supported in the private communications I received from many of the well-known field researchers in sociology on the occasion of reviewing the first draft of this manuscript. As one might expect, one of the more perceptive observations in this respect came from Howard S. Becker. He said that field workers, like many others, were often interested in "keeping their options open"—and that's why reports of field research are generally so impersonal and bland.

5. For a historical analysis of these matters, see Robert W. Friedricks, *A Sociology of Sociology.* New York: The Free Press, 1970.

6. These observations are detailed and analyzed more fully in my unpublished paper titled "The Social Meanings of Social Science Research," 1972.

7. This was the context in which one of my intimates expressed his thinking that one supervisor's attempts to have the observer removed from the setting during the tenth month of the investigation were epiphenomenal to the ongoing "one-upsmanship game" between the two supervisors.

8. Ernst Cassirer, *The Philosophy of Symbolic Forms,* vol. III, *The Phenomenology of Knowledge.* New Haven, Conn.: Yale University Press, 1957, p. 306.

9. Aaron Cicourel, *Method and Measurement in Sociology*. New York: The Free Press, 1964, pp. 54–66.

10. Especially see Erving Goffman, *The Presentation of Self in Everyday Life*. Garden City, N.Y.: Doubleday, 1959.

11. See S. M. Miller, "The Participant Observer and 'Over-Rapport,'" *American Sociological Review,* 18 (1953): 97–9.

12. It should be underscored that I am referring here only to what the social workers defined as sanctions; whatever the various welfare clients might have perceived or experienced as sanctionable or a sanction is an entirely different issue altogether.

13. In his long-term research investigation of the police, Jerome Skolnick concluded that he had been systematically excluded from witnessing those actions which could plausibly be interpreted as police brutality, violations of another's rights, and the like. See his *Justice without Trial*. New York: Wiley, 1966.

Chapter 6

Fusions of Thinking and Feeling in Field Research

PERSONAL RELATIONS of trust are necessary to obtain a truthful understanding of others. Chapter 4 stresses the importance of this for the conduct of field research. In everyday life, however, we seldom give much thought to it, except perhaps on those relatively infrequent occasions when our expectations are rendered problematic by some out-of-the-ordinary event. Certainly there are few of us who go about analyzing trust as a distinct topic for study in our everyday lives. Indeed, if we did go about doing this, others might begin to think we were a bit odd, at best, or perhaps acting insincerely. When one is concerned with the observational methods of a research project, however, and especially the influences of these methods on the truthfulness of the information one collects, analyzing a topic such as this is necessary. This means that methodological accounts of sociological field research will inevitably foster imagery of instrumentality; that is, they will implicitly paint a picture of the field worker as an iron-willed, steel-nerved, cunning Machiavellian manipulator of the symbolic tools of everyday discourse. For a given inves-

145

tigation, an observer may have been personally motivated or inspired by the hopes that the research would be a step toward the realization of some abstract ideal, such as advancing knowledge, bettering mankind, alleviating human suffering, or solving social problems. But teleological justifications such as these are methodologically irrelevant. For methodological purposes, the important ones are the *how* questions, not the *why* questions. This traditional emphasis is considered justified because it is only when an observer is able to specify how the observations were made that they will be considered capable of independent verification by other observers. When we recall the intimate linkages between what are considered scientific facts and the methods used to produce them, then the strong instrumentality emphasis of methodological writings is easier to understand. But we should be careful always to keep in mind that these overrationalized methodological accounts are never the whole story about the research.

It is possible to review the methodological literature with an eye to discovering how social scientists conceive their actual conduct as scientists, that is, their implied model of competent scientific inquiry. When this is done, two major emphases are unmistakable. First, an implied model of rational scientific decision making consistently emerges in this literature. For example, unlike many of the rest of us, who sometimes do things and then figure out "reasons" for them after the fact, scientists appear always to know what course of action they will elect prior to engaging in any actual conduct. The decision may change, of course, as additional information becomes available, but these alterations of research practice are also made on rational grounds. The second major emphasis is the very strong one on thinking and other cognitive operations by scientific observers. Most of us have an intuitive understanding that our personal feelings are very important ingredients of our everyday practical affairs. There is a vast range of human feelings, and most of us understand the importance of sexual desire, love, hate, resentment, infatuation, exhaustion, and all the others. These are often the prime movers of our daily actions. But the methodological literature contains very few references to the writers' feelings. On the whole, it is impossible to review the literature about methods in the social sciences without reaching the conclusion that "having feelings" is like an incest taboo in sociological research.

It isn't correct to say that the topic of personal feelings has been completely ignored by those who have done scientific research. There are some exceptions. One example is William Whyte's expression of embarrassment, even fear, upon being threatened with physical harm as a result of an inappropriate advance toward one of the girls in a street-corner tavern at the beginning of his research.[1] Another example is Rosalie Wax's expression of sympathy for the Japanese–Americans interned in the relocation camps during the Second World War, and her reflection that getting drunk on sake decreases one's ability to record field notes.[2] A third example is Donald Roy's partial explanation of why he has continued his research studies with labor-union organizing campaigns for over several decades: ". . . I must admit that conversing with working stiffs is for me a matter of taking the line of least resistance."[3] But exceptions to the general assertion above are few in number. More importantly, the remarks about the observer's feelings that are made tend to be presented in an anecdotal fashion and not considered seriously.

There is one scholar, however, who has seriously considered the fusions of thinking and feeling in sociological research. This is Kurt Wolff. He addresses this issue while reviewing the anthropological and sociological research literature, and as a major focus of his reflections on his field-research experiences at Loma spanning two decades.[4] Reviewing the methodological writings, Wolff analyzes the common field-research phenomenon of the observer's transforming all affective and interactional elements of an action into *cognitive* problems. He writes:

That is to say, the relevance of what is observed is transformed into theoretical relevance, and the relevance of the observer into theoretical interest. Even the field worker's confusion has a purely theoretical meaning; when he writes, "I did not clearly see any reason why I should enquire into one matter rather than another," there is no affective or interactive component in his meaning: interaction and affect are limited for him to interaction with and affect for cognitive problems, although they are more purely limited and more passionate, more unconditional within these limits than anywhere else in a community study that I know of. It is as if Bateson's humanity was absent from relations with the people he lived with and studied and had been wholly absorbed in his burning theoretical concern.[5]

The Bateson study to which Wolff refers is, according to his analysis, characterized by the transformation of all affective and interactional elements into cognitive problems. But he concludes that just the opposite occurred during his five field studies at Loma between 1940 and 1960. Wolff reflects:

It was years before I understood what had happened to me; I had fallen through the web of "culture patterns" and assorted conceptual meshes into the chaos of *love;* I was looking everywhere, famished, with a "ruthless glance." Despite admonitions to be selective and form hypotheses that would tell me what to select, I was not and did not. Another thing I sensed was that I was not content with the probable but wanted to *know;* and I thought I might *know* if, instead of looking for culture patterns, for instance, I looked directly—not through the lens of *any* received notion but the adequate lens that would come out of my being in Loma. "Culture pattern," indeed any conceptual scheme, had come to strike me as something learned *outside* Loma that I would import, impose, and that had been imposed on me. Instead, I was busy, even panicky at times, observing, ruminating, recording as best I could. Everything, I felt, was important, although the ways in which it was important would yet have to become clear. But then there was also the fear that I should be overwhelmed by the mass of my notes; I could not possibly keep in mind all the veins, lodes, and outcroppings of that growing mountain of typescript.[6]

The "chaos of love" Wolff subsequently conceptualizes as "surrender." There are several distinct dimensions of the meaning of surrender for Wolff, but he argues that the essential, or core, meaning is "cognitive love." He clearly states, however, that this conception represents a *retrospective* interpretation. He writes:

> I can give no excerpts from my field notes that would exemplify or analyze these meanings. The reason is, as I have said, that I had not surrendered to Loma beyond the low degree of being most tensely alert to what was going on around me; what was going on in myself had not yet begun to announce itself as relevant to my enterprise. Hence there is no record—or at least none that I could present in a brief excerpt—of self-observation which would show involvement, identification, or hurt.[7]

Wolff's reflections on his field-research experiences are presented here in some detail because this is *the one instance* in the methodological writings where the fusions of thinking and feeling are considered seriously, where they are treated as other than anecdotes. He expresses a deep sense that his feelings were a very crucial part of the project, even one of the fundamental determinants of what he the observer *saw* and reported as findings of the inquiry. And yet no records were made on these phenomena at the time. There is no record to assess their influence, if any, on the validity of the observational data. And all we have is a retrospective interpretation of a *cognitive* love for the members of Loma—no lust, feelings of sensuality, hatred, disgust, anger, ecstasy, bewilderment, or even stomach pains, but a cognitive love. Thus, in the one instance where the fusions of thinking and feeling are seriously addressed as one of the problematic features of actual research conduct, our instruction is to believe that on those rare occasions when a scientific research observer feels, he only does so *thinkingly!*

My field-research experiences at the welfare offices lend some limited support to Wolff's conception of cognitive love but also show that the fusions of thinking and feeling in social research are much more complicated than this. Before elaborating on that conclusion, however, a few more personal remarks are in order. Analyzing feelings or their relevance to the issues of objectivity in the social sciences was not considered at the beginning of the project. The very idea of doing this never entered my mind. In candor I will have to say that a substantial portion of my field observations involved features of the naive rationalistic perspective mentioned previously. Furthermore, I will have to partially associate my observational and recording practices with Wolff's recording omissions as he reflects on them. Even though I initially intended an investigation of the research process itself, my voluminous records contain relatively few explicit notes on my personal feelings. I do have some records on them, but even some of these are expressed in an unusual manner. This will become clear in the subsequent pages.

It's impossible for me to say precisely when it occurred to me to consider that the relations between thoughts and feelings might be relevant for understanding everyday, practical action. I can say, however, that my first thoughts about this possibility concerned the social casework done by the CWS social workers, not social research. The possibility didn't occur to me for many months. And then it was only after a rather lengthy period when I studied this issue with respect to the practice of social casework that the relevance of the relations between thoughts and feelings to social research occurred to me. To put this in a different perspective, I can say the CWS social workers instructed me in some matters about which my teachers, mentors, and professional associates were ignorant—or, more charitably, some matters they considered pedagogically irrelevant.

After three years of reviewing the observational records and writing and reflecting, my analyses lead to the conclusion that there are several distinct ways the personal feelings of the observer become fused with the rational cognitions of the inquiry. It is not appropriate to think of "levels" of the feelings, but there is a certain ascendancy to them, ranging as they do from the most immediate to the rather remote. The major theoretical and methodological questions raised by this issue of feelings all ask for an assessment of their influence on what are subsequently reported as the findings of the empirical study. For some, it is relatively easy to judge the influence of feelings as negligible or trivial. For others, the assessment is more difficult. Materials presented in the remainder of this chapter highlight these issues.

BEHIND RATIONAL SELF-PRESENTATION

In many if not most cases the first way an observer's feelings become intertwined with his observations is through various anxieties experienced at the beginning of a research project. Even though the relatively few notations of the observer's feelings scattered in the methodological writings are usually presented as anecdotes, it is still possible to read between the lines and infer a recognition that the very beginning of a field-research project is frequently attended by feelings of anxiety. While there is only one report on the first days in the field as such, many writers have mentioned their initial experiences upon entree.[8] Without actually reporting their own experiences, many others advise hopeful field researchers to delay recording any observations or making other notes until several weeks of the project have passed, when the anxieties subside.[9] The beginning of the field observations and the initial contacts with those in the research setting are widely recognized as intertwined with private fears, apprehensions, feelings of ignorance, confusion, incompetence, and incomprehension, and so forth.

In my field research in the welfare offices, I experienced all these feelings at the beginning, and some periodically thereafter, and mine were complicated by distinct physical manifestations of various kinds. When I returned to my apartment at the end of the very first day of field work at the Lakeside office, several of the blood vessels in my nose broke. Blood spewed forth at a frightening rate onto the floor and the carpet. I was taken to the emergency room of a local hospital by one of the social workers I had met that day. The doctor said the event was "inexplicable." Upon coming home again, I recorded field notes for *seven hours*. In retrospect, that also appears to be a reflection of my feelings of anxiety, apprehension, worries about doing a good job, and the like. For the remainder of my initial stay at the offices in the Northern Metropolitan County, the physical manifestations of my anxieties were not as explosively dramatic as on the first day. But intense indirect manifestations, such as by the demented recording ritual, continued.

Chapter 3 mentioned what occurred when I addressed the joint meeting of the social workers of the two CWS units at the Metro office to explain the purposes of the research. A few of the social workers departed this meeting with the idea that I could still be a spy from the governor's office, but several others thought my lack of composure while receiving the accusations constituted some evidence that the charges of spying might not have been warranted. Behind my tenuous self-presentation there were genuine anxieties and worries. My anxieties eventually diminished, but some remained for a considerable length of time. I recorded the following excerpt from my field notes about six weeks after beginning at Metro.

I'm not sure whether these comments will ultimately have any relevance whatsoever, but I guess I'll add a couple of remarks to the day's field notes to record some of my personal thoughts which I haven't made any note of before. I've been going down to [Metro] for nearly six weeks now, and even though I probably appear cucumber-cool to everybody down there, I am, for the most part, scared to death of some of those people, and in many cases I don't know any good reasons for this. Every morning around seven forty-five, as I'm driving to the office, I begin to get this pain in the left side of my back, and the damn thing stays there usually until around eleven, when I've made my daily plans for accompanying one of the workers. Since nearly all of the workers remain in the office until around eleven or twelve, and since there's only one extra chair in the two units, and no extra desks as yet, those first two or three hours are sheer agony for me every damn day. Trying to be busy without hassling any one worker too much is like playing Chinese checkers, hopping to and fro, from here to there, with no place to hide. But I guess that the biggest thing that keeps gnawing at me is Bonnie's reaction to my presence in the office. Man, if I would've had any idea at all before I began this damn project that a field researcher could possibly cause anyone so much grief, you can bet that I wouldn't be here.

I recorded a voluminous amount of notes during the early months, comparatively at least. I think I recorded even more of them then than later, notwithstanding the advice of the traditional research literature to the contrary. As I subsequently reviewed these early notes, I found them not especially valuable ones, in terms either of description or of insight. But it is not at all clear that this resulted from my feelings of anxiety. In retrospect, it is just as plausible to think the notes trivial, naive, and often mistaken character resulted from my ignorance of the setting and its tasks, official rules, names, terminology, and the like.

Field workers generally agree that the initial anxious feelings eventually subside, but this does not necessarily mean all goes smoothly thereafter. The following excerpt from my notes was recorded during the tenth week at Metro. It describes my reactions to a talk with a worker called Buzz.

Also had a talk with Buzz this afternoon. I began by asking him what had happened recently with the kids at the Young foster home, where we were last week. Buzz began his account by saying "Oh wow, J.J., you wouldn't believe how bad I blew it," and then he proceeded to describe the details of what he called his own ignorance, unprofessional conduct, erroneous judgments, sentimental and sloppy thinking, bad social casework, and so on. Now I'll admit that I don't know all there is to know about social workers or social casework, but I sure as hell know enough about it to know that all the examples he cited from this case wouldn't be similarly defined by *any* other social worker, that there isn't a social worker in the world who would see that as unprofessional conduct, or anything else. The account would've been implausible from nearly any worker, but it's [especially] implausible coming from Buzz. He's one of the brightest guys I've met so far. . . . It's fairly obvious he was giving me some kind of short-con this afternoon, although I'll be damned if I have any idea why. The thing today really got to me. After taking leave of the situation, I walked out of the office and over to the parking lot whereupon I proceeded to break into a cold sweat, felt weak-knee'd and nauseous.

The excerpt gives another illustration of private feelings and their physical manifestations. Interestingly, it also shows the researcher, in this case myself, taking leave of the situation to hide these from others. Not wanting to give any of the social workers an opportunity for developing a "fatal insight" about my apparently rational self-presentation, I make an exit to the nearby parking lot, where I try to reconstruct a rational appearance. Also implicit in the excerpt is an indication that relatively early in the research I was oriented to a "normal" state of affairs at the office. It was recorded only because the event it depicts breaches prior anticipation of "normality," even though the comments themselves show no awareness that this is why I recorded it. Because there wasn't any such awareness. The excerpt is an excellent illustration of the self-organizing and essentially *conservative* nature of the observer's rationalistic perspective. When confronted with an account conflicting with prior anticipation or other knowledge, the observer reflexively tries to conserve the foundations of his rationalistic vision by treating the appearance of conflict as epiphenomenal to some "reason," albeit one that is not as yet known.

Apart from the initial moments of anxiety at the beginning of any new research, the early portions of the investigation engage the researcher's deeper feelings. As suggested above, this process may involve stirring up one's commonsensical and taken-for-granted presuppositions about "normal" social reality and rationality. Also involved are those basic ideas others have termed "world hypotheses" and "domain assumptions." [10] The first anxious moments are likely to be unimportant for the research observations, at least as compared with one's primordial feelings about what reality is. The latter are likely to be fundamental determinants of what one sees when doing observation.

WHEN THE RATIONAL APPEARANCES CRACK

The previous comments document the possibility of a gap between one's rational self-presentation and one's private feelings. Furthermore, the point was made that the maintenance of a rational appearance is a self-organizing and conservative enterprise of daily life. The following accounts of two separate events illustrate the problematic nature of the enterprise.

The event to be discussed first occurred relatively late in the observations at Metro. The account is reminiscent of the folk account of the kid caught with his hand in the cookie jar.

I'm not sure I've recorded any notes about this, but ever since they added those partitions dividing all of the supervisors' offices in half, I've been ducking into the interviewing rooms on the other side of Frank's and Mary's offices to eavesdrop. . . . Well, today, because I got a lot of good dope from a discussion in the coffee room with Barrie and her gang, I ducked into one of the rooms in order to write a couple of pages of notes. About three or four minutes after I had been in the interviewing room, I heard Sherri begin a conversation with Mary on the other side of the partition. But, after hearing some of the opening remarks which indicated they were talking about Sherri's recent crisis with her boyfriend, I just ignored the conversation and went on recording my field notes. Wow, I should've paid attention to the talking, at least enough to know when they'd stopped. When I finished my notes I stepped out of the interviewing room, and who should I meet walking around the corner. Yep, you guessed it. [It was Sherri.] My heart must have hit the floor. I felt like Portnoy must have felt when his mother was knocking on the bathroom door. I think I tried to forge the appearance of a smile, but I'll bet it was obvious as hell that I was really shaking. I somehow managed to make it to the back door, and lost my breakfast out by the railroad tracks.

One noteworthy feature of this out-of-the-ordinary event is, again, the relation of my private feelings to physical signs, which one might plausibly interpret in this case as an index of the socially sanctionable nature of social interaction that had occurred.[11] Notice also that even though my reactions to the event were serious enough to produce physical signs, my notes fail to record what the actual feelings were. Whatever feelings existed, they were not verbally expressed, and this could be because they were inarticulable, unexpressible ones, like many of our feelings. This underscores the great difficulties of understanding one's day-to-day, ordinary feelings, and their relevance to one's perceptions or actions.

The next event is depicted in some detail by my field notes. They record my feelings about an incident occurring one afternoon at the local Juvenile Court. The case involved a determination of the legal custody of a four-year-old boy, David. David's mother had officially relinquished her first four children for adoption several years earlier. But since his birth David had been "unofficially placed in an unlicensed foster home," the official euphemistic vernacular for saying David's mother gave him to someone else. Such a practice is relatively common in the poorer areas of the city, much to the consternation of the Foster Home Licensing officials, it should be noted.[12] David had been living with the Smiths for the last four years. On this day, the case came to court because David's mother wanted to take David away from the Smiths to send him to Oklahoma so that her relatives there could receive more money from the local welfare agency. Incidentally, this is not very common, but it does occur now and then. As the notes will show, the Smiths had obviously come to regard David as their own son.

> . . . however, neither I nor all of the persons who had come to testify in the Smiths' behalf were allowed to witness the proceedings. Even though I wasn't allowed inside the courtroom, I decided to wait around in the lobby until the case had been concluded. I waited both minutes.

The reference to waiting both minutes is literal, not ironic, and this time element is typical for juvenile courts, not extraordinary.[13] The reference to waiting both minutes masks my private feelings of indignation and incomprehension about the unintelligible bases on which such consequential decisions are frequently made.[14] I say this, it should be understood, after having engaged in conscientious and concerted efforts to understand the Juvenile Court situation from the various perspectives of the different participants. Returning to the David Smith case:

> As the parties allowed into the Juvenile Court proceedings re-emerged into the lobby, the following events transpired. The first one through the door was Mrs. Smith's brother, a gargantuan man of about forty-five years, about six-four, with a neck like a circus strong man. Was wearing one of those checkered shirts like lumberjacks wear, under his overalls. At the scale, he'd probably weigh in about two hundred fifty pounds. He was really broken up, crying heavily and pounding his fist against the wall. David's foster mother, Mrs. Smith, presented the appearance of one who had gone absolutely hysterical. Her bulky frame was being carried through the door on the shoulders of her long time friend on one side, and her next door neighbor on the other. At the top of her lungs she demanded that divine intervention make its appearance on the scene in the name of justice. She called for God, and asked for intervention to correct what she very obviously thought was a miscarriage of justice. She then turned on David's natural mother and threatened physical violence, but was restrained by her two friends and a burly Sheriff. She screamed

that justice had not been done, that David's mother did not deserve to have him returned as she had not bothered to even visit him once in four years, even though she lived only one block from the Smiths. She claimed that her life was now meaningless and not worth living any more. She was ushered outside by her friends, and they stood out on the sidewalk for a couple of minutes. During this time David began crying and screaming, claiming that he did not want to be returned to his natural mother, that he didn't want to go to Oklahoma. He said he hated his natural mother and didn't want to leave his foster home. Within a couple of minutes, after Mrs. Smith's brother had stopped crying, he threatened to kill David's mother on the spot, and re-entered the building to make good on his threat, whereupon he was almost literally smothered by what seemed like five hundred onlookers and the entire Sheriff's Department, persons obviously sensing that his utterance was not what is called "an idle threat." He was finally "ushered" out of the lobby, and he and his sister and friends and neighbors adjourned to the parking lot where they cried and hugged each other with what appeared to be a great deal of anguish and suffering.

David, of course, exerted all efforts to join his loved ones, and had to be restrained by the Sheriff's officer in the lobby. The scene proved too much for those onlookers in the lobby, and the guards, probation officers and receptionist began crying profusely. Betty [the social worker] also appeared visibly shaken and ran to her car crying.

The notes refer to Mrs. Smith's brother as "almost . . . smothered" by a (greatly exaggerated) number of onlookers. They did not include myself. I was one of the few who did not join the restraining action. As well as I can remember, I just stood there, stunned by the unfolding scenario. The conclusion depicts my reactions.

And how did the cool, objective, calculatingly rational social scientist react to all of this? Having quickly analyzed all of the formally rational courses of action open to me, and feeling confident that I had controlled for all spurious relations, I also began to cry. As we say in the trade, I presented the appearance of one who had lost all self-control. And then, when alone on the grounds of the juvenile facility several minutes later, I presented the appearance of a formally rational [expletive deleted] social scientist beating his [deleted] fist against a tree. Shortly after that, I doubled over and puked my guts out. What am I doing here anyway?! To hell with the appearance of sociology and the horse it rode in on!

After these events I returned home and spent most of the evening crying. The field notes were not recorded in the heat of the moment, then, but the following day; this was one of the few times I didn't record notes on the day of the observation. Notice that even given this elapsed time, the field notes do not explicitly say what the feelings were in the situation. Even though this was a very emotional event, the actual feelings are glossed and masked with cynicism. By adopting the observer's stance here, it is possible to read between the lines and conclude it was "more human" in the situation itself to cry, lose self-control, or whatever. But the later notes, instead of recording a relatively straightforward expression of one's sense of injustice, feelings of sympathy, outrage, or whatever the feelings actually were in the situation, gloss the tensions between primordial, gut-level feelings and rational thoughts by cynical phrases such as "presented the appearance" and "controlled for all spurious relations." One might propose that I was just an incompetent recorder or, worse, lacked aesthetic sensibilities, and there might be an element of truth in the proposal. But as we recall Kurt Wolff's analysis of the common tendency for research observers to transform all interactive and affective elements into *cognitive* problems, it is wiser to conceive the tensions between thinking and feeling as necessary and inevitable ones. They are necessary and inevitable ones, that is, as long as one retains a moral commitment to the observations. To observe sociologically means that one *deliberately cedes* experiencing the things in themselves to the members of the setting; observation entails seeing phenomena as "exhibits" of the things in themselves. If one elects to do observation sociologically, there is and can be no other way. In practice, of course, the distinction breaks down slightly. There is actually a mixture, and we bob in and out, to and fro. We participate, observe, experience, record, pause for reflection, and then return for more of the same. But the field researcher's valued commitment to observing and recording notes on the events of daily life means that there will always be, to some irreducible degree, a transformation of the actual experiences into something other than what they were in reality. There is a sizable body of writings on the phenomenon of going native in anthropological and sociological field-research literature.[15] These writings attest the problematic nature of the commitment and the existence of other plausible alternatives. That we make and are made up of the phenomena we seek to understand is the irremediable paradox of our enterprise.

When viewed in the broader perspective of the entire field investigation, the David Smith case was methodologically trivial and substantively unimportant. Personally, however, the experience had, and continues to have, a lasting biographical relevance. I had spent a decade of absolutist commitment to the causes of the American Civil Liberties Union. As I periodically paused to reflect on the David Smith case, the ironic contrasts were too obvious and painfully evident. Had the ACLU filed an *amicus curiae* brief in this case, it would have promoted the very outcome which resulted in my profound sense of injustice. The event was one of several leading to changes in my thinking about legalistic and other rule-governed remedies. My ACLU membership elapsed sometime later, and I did not renew it. And that was no small decision, for me at least.

FEELINGS AND PERSONAL INVOLVEMENTS

The overformalized rationalistic instrumentality which appears as the public account of one's "methods" is never the whole story of the research. Our discussions to this point document two ways an observer's personal feelings become fused with the rational accounts—through the initial anxieties at the start of the research and one's gut-level reactions to the situation at hand. A third way, decidedly more important, involves one's ongoing personal relations with the persons in the setting where the research is conducted. All field investigations which penetrate the rational appearances of the public front of a setting, which involve relations of trust with the individuals there to obtain a truthful, empathetic, valid, and reliable understanding of the actions occurring there, will inevitably involve complicated personal feelings between the observer and the members. Instead of being dependent on one's gut-level reactions to an immediate situation, many of these feelings are of a transsituational character, and some accrue glacially over time, perhaps without explicit awareness. But this does not mean these dimensions of feeling are less primordial than the others or that they necessarily transcend the gut level because of the time involved. In substantive terms, some of the inhabitants of this realm of feeling are sympathy, love, hate, friendship, resentment, admiration, respect, infatuation, identification, and dislike. Such feelings are the meaningful stuff of which the problems of over-rapport and going native are made, to use the euphemisms of the field-research writings.

The complicated feelings between an observer and the persons among whom the investigation is conducted may involve, as Kurt Wolff has taught us, cognitive elements, even a cognitive love. Based on my reflections, the conception of cognitive love precisely characterizes my feelings toward one of the CWS social workers at Metro, and one other worker at another office. It cannot be said that the CWS worker at Metro and I immediately hit it off as a result of some personal compatibility. He was the one who lodged the first accusation that I might be a spy from the governor's office at the initial meeting of the two CWS units. For the first couple of months our interactions with one another were cordial but cool. Eventually we became friends, largely as a consequence of our generally compatible personalities, demeanors, past experiences, interests, and so forth. Personally I liked him and felt certain about communicating such sentiments, and he responded accordingly. In retrospect, this particular friendship might have been anticipated, even though it wasn't. It might have been anticipated because, in the terms used in the traditional field-research literature to categorize types of informants one is likely to find in a given setting, this CWS worker was a "natural," that is, one of those rare reflective individuals capable of very insightful analyses of daily events.[16] As we were around each other more and more, he gradually became even more inclined to see his practical CWS actions as exhibits for analysis. By the end of my stay at Metro he referred to these analyses as *his* participant-observation research, and it is my judgment that I successfully "turned him out" as an analyst of everyday affairs. On several occasions I told him it was unfortunate that he was not the observer for the field investigation of CWS. And I meant it. A number of the insightful ideas I subsequently reported were, quite frankly, stolen from him.

In addition to being a natural, this CWS social worker happened to occupy *the* key position in the two CWS units with respect to information control and case-load referral. Also, he single-handedly altered or subverted several existing official policies or practices directly affecting the character of the CWS work at Metro. Several of these actions were clandestine, and others patently illegal.[17] This may have been one of the reasons for his initial apprehension about admitting an outsider access to the official public secrets. In short, it would have been impossible to obtain a valid understanding of what occurred at Metro CWS without befriending this worker. In this respect, I consider my friendship with him as very fortuitous for the research.

Wolff's abstract definition of the core meaning of "surrender" as "cognitive love" does make some sense, then. On other counts, however, the idealization fails miserably in telling us how affective and interactional elements of action are involved in the research process, and hence distorts our understanding. Conspicuously absent is any mention of the nonrational grounds of some of our pettier feelings. Take the two freeze-outs I encountered during the field observations at Metro. One was the girl who told her friends she was "horrified" by my presence. I agonized over this situation for months and months, resolutely rejecting others' explanations of it by invoking some typification of her personality, continually thinking of ways to put her at ease, and worrying about what I must be doing wrong. What emerged out of all this was a private irrational fear of her. I *still* don't know why it came, but the feelings of fear were real ones.

My relations with the second freeze-out mellowed over time, but they were none too friendly at best. In contrast to the first instance, where my private feelings could be said to have epitomized an Adlai Stevenson consciousness almost until the end, my private feelings about this fellow were less charitable. Frankly, I thought he was a "betty," although I think I successfully masked that sentiment during the research.

Petty feelings emerged in other situations. On one or two occasions I just got bored and fabricated some excuse to escape for a desired respite from boredom. As noted earlier, on one occasion an older woman directed moral indignation at me because I had "lowered myself" by going with one of the male social workers to throw a glorious drunk at several infamous brothels of a neighboring community. I spoke deferentially in my response to her, but my private feelings consisted of "deleted expletives." I wasn't in the mood for that kind of social wrath at the time. Wolff's emphasis on the cognitive character of one's affect ignores all these petty feelings, but they are all only too recognizable in our everyday actions.

The experiences of my social welfare research included several friendships. Some originated before the research, and some have continued for years afterward. Others came to bloom during the observations but have atrophied over time. Only on one occasion did I have a sense that a friendship presented a problem for the research. This situation involved the personal struggle between one CWS supervisor and the CWS social worker who was legally blind. The supervisor didn't think blind persons should be in CWS. She set out to build a case against him, a preliminary to having him dismissed. Because of his reliance on a paid driver for transportation, the blind worker was caught in a bind. He feared his presence in the office during the working day would be used to constitute part of the case against him. He solicited my assistance as his cover for a period of about three weeks. Without hesitation I agreed. This meant that I went with him on many more home calls during this time than I otherwise would have done. The problematic character of this, for me at least, consisted of the conflict between this course of action and the specific welfare activities I wanted to concentrate on at the time. It is doubtful whether my actions introduced any additional elements of selectivity into the research observations, but with different options I would have chosen otherwise.

A claim that field research involves feelings of friendship is one that deserves considered reflection. One issue raised by this is the possibility of a conflict between one's personal feelings and a rational course of action intended to effect the best observational results. This issue is raised by the comments in the preceding paragraph. If or when such a conflict occurs, it is incumbent on the observer to use his sociological competencies to evaluate the effects. But there are other potential conflicts inherent in friendships, and these are little appreciated. The most obvious possibility is that of a conflict between the substantively rational sentiments of friendship and a formally rational body of codified rules such as legal statutes.

Having spent much of my time for the past decade lingering in and about official state bureaucracies, notably universities, welfare agencies, and military commands, it is very difficult for me to believe there are many adults who are *not* technically guilty of periodic violations of official rules, such as laws. Illegal drug use, for example, is very common in these settings.[18] And yet one almost never hears of an instance where one colleague calls in the police on another or uses the "hot line" to Washington. Unauthorized sexual liaisons are frequent. Some members don't even know what the official rules are about these, and not surprisingly; the rules are rarely invoked.[19] Playing around with the entries on official records and reports is common. These public secrets rarely inspire moral indignation. The potential for conflicts between the absolutism of the formally rational legal codes and the moral pluralism of substantively rational family, friendship, and colleague sentiments is obvious in these settings. When a conflict actually occurs, the members invariably elect a moral or ethical view over a legalistic one, at least with respect to *their own* or their friends' actions. This would be no news to many parents; the game is typically "no holds barred" when one is called to the police station in the middle of the night to extricate a son or daughter from the clutches of the officials. My personal thinking has been undeniably colored by these kinds of experiences. But I am also aware that the situation is very different in other settings. Among the BaMbuti in Africa, for example, the possibility of such conflicts would not arise because of the homogeneity and uncodified nature of their moral sentiments.[20] Even in our own teeming, conglomerated societies there are pockets of moral isolation where it is possible to live without dealing with these complexities on a day-to-day basis, such as the Amish communities of northern Indiana and many university laboratories.

I am aware of many others who do not share my views on this subject.[21] Whether or not my suppositions are correct, however, if one were to view my field-research conduct in the welfare agencies from a legalistic perspective, it would be seen that my actions involved complicity in, or "guilty knowledge" of, literally hundreds and hundreds of illegal activities. The relevant legal categorizations would include being an accessory before and after the fact of an illegal act, misprision of felonies and misdemeanors, obstructing justice, and others. From my understanding of the field-research literature, but especially from my many conversations and "debriefings" with colleagues in sociology, it was, and still is, inconceivable to me to report such actions to the legal authorities.[22] I regarded my ethical position on this particular issue as an absolute one; I was prepared to go to jail before violating the confidentiality of the research information.[23] And I still feel that way. To put this in the vernacular popularized by the Watergate follies, I was, and am, prepared to "stonewall it" to the end. It comes as a surprise to me, then, to learn that this is not the position taken by other sociological researchers.[24]

Observers of all kinds have remarked about the strength and pervasiveness of sexual desire for aeons. Modern psychology elevates this tidbit of common-sense knowledge to scientific status and calls the desire a drive. And yet when one reviews the methodological writings in the social sciences, the implicit instruction is to believe one of two things about this: either one must be a eunuch to conduct scientific research, or, in the vein of Wolff's argument, the desires of scientists involve only (or primarily) cognitive elements. My research experiences, and my other experiences, do not support this naive view. One example (although I shall mask the specific details) is a series of events that occurred near the end of my investigations. They involved what has been called the eternal triangle for centuries in literature, the third party being one of the inside informants for the research and a close personal friend of my wife. The resolution involved feelings of bitterness, betrayal, hate, resentment, and shattered friendships. It produced a severe crisis for me personally and delayed the writing of the research reports. The situation involved a considerable amount of "hurt," which is one of the elements of Wolff's definition of surrender. But it would be pure casuistry for me to consider the prime mover of these events as the *cognitive* element of social action!

In one sense, the present discussion only brings out in the open some of the public secrets of scientific conduct which many have understood for a long time. John Lofland aptly captures this common understanding, and some of the reasons for masking one's research account. He writes:

> One of my mentors has commented that what typically goes into "how the study was done" are "the second worst things that

happened." I am inclined to believe that his generalization is correct. What person with an eye to his future, and who wishes others to think positively of him, is going to relate anything about himself that is morally or professionally discrediting in any important way? This is especially the case since field work tends to be performed by youngish persons who have longer futures to think about and less security about the shape of those futures. We delude ourselves if we expect very many field workers actually to "tell all" in print.[25]

During the Watergate investigations, our brother sociologist Richard M. Nixon coined a phrase which expresses Lofland's observations in a more parsimonious fashion. When his aides were called on by others to reveal the methodological protocol of certain past events, as it were, he advised a "limited hangout." My experiences and reflections tend to support the wisdom of sociologists Lofland and Nixon. I think the best we can expect from the methodological literature is a limited hang-out.

The complicated fusions of feelings and rational thoughts which become intertwined in any scientific investigation raise two major theoretical questions. The first is whether some form of direct participation by an observer with the members of the social group being studied introduces any greater degree of bias or error into an investigation than would obtain from an observer's reliance on his own common-sense thinking based on no direct personal involvement. The evidence on this is mixed, but it is clear that a "detached" investigation based on no direct participation contains a great potential for not being true. Others have previously addressed this question, so it will not be dealt with in detail here.[26]

The second major question is related to the issue of establishing relations of trust in anthropological and sociological field research. Many analysts agree that trusting relations are the essential ingredients if the research report is to be a true one. The question is whether the sentiments resulting from the observer's personal relations with the individuals in the setting necessarily mean that the research report will be biased. This does seem to be a distinct possibility, but there is clearly no *a priori* reason for thinking that it will necessarily occur. These personal sentiments would appear to become a potentially biasing feature of the research when the observer's intentions to *empathize* with the individuals in the setting, that is, to truthfully understand the situation from the actors' perspective, become transformed into a *sympathetic* stance. A sympathetic stance exists where the observer takes the side of, or promotes the perspective of, the group he studies.[27] Such a distinction is often less than clear-cut. The understanding of this leads some analysts to advise the wisdom of reading all field-research reports with an eye to its tenuous nature.[28] The same understanding exists in common-sense thought. It is commonly expressed by the remark that one always looks at one's loved ones with rose-colored glasses.

FEELINGS ABOUT HOME

Perhaps the single most important stimulus for a field researcher's ability to honor the distinction between empathy and sympathy in his observations and analyses is his simultaneous relations with professional colleagues. Generally speaking, a field worker has a foot in two different camps at the same time—ongoing relations with those in the research setting and ongoing relations with sociological friends, teachers, advisers, and peers. A researcher is able to move back and forth between these simultaneous roles. Sociological colleagues, through informal conversations, seminars, debriefings, and the like, may serve to "keep the researcher honest," that is, as a check against the possibility of taking a sympathetic stance in the research observations. It goes without saying, of course, that many ideas for the research will emerge from such contacts. There are several practical (even utilitarian) elements about these collegial relations which are necessary for the completion of any project, and the colleagues do provide a check on the objectivity of the research in many cases, and, in a fundamentally important sense, this is where the researcher "lives." His colleagues and friends are the ones who shower or withhold those statements of praise, probity, or damnation out of which all of us try to put together some conception of a social self. This is home. Whether one stays with the project to the end or says "to hell with it" is often dependent on these personal ties. This is another way one's personal feelings become fused with the rational cognitions of the enterprise.

The same congeries of feelings which may come into play between the observer and the individuals in the research setting may emerge in one's collegial relations. These personal ties are typically alluded to in the introduction, preface, or opening footnotes of a work. They cut across all known categories of theoretical perspectives, methodological programs, political beliefs, substantive interests, and value commitments. There is even a traditional format used to acknowledge these ties. It consists of mentioning one's colleagues and then absolving them of any moral responsibility for what are to be reported as the findings of the research. This is done in virtually all books on sociological work. For example:

> It goes without saying that [my colleague] is in no way to be held responsible for what follows. While there may be honor among thieves as well as among sociologists of knowledge, some crimes are committed together and some separately.[29]

The traditional format is a quaint holdover from the past. It promotes a moral perspective honored only on such ritualistic occasions as the writing of prefaces; it distorts the actual truth. It is also poor sociology of knowledge, and many of the personal reflections of scientists show that few really take such statements seriously anyway, at least in theoretical terms.[30] The tradition does point up, however, that all rationalistic sociological accounts are quintessentially *social* enterprises. As with some other forms of "crime," we would probably be well advised to think of the moral responsibility as collective rather than individual.

Trying to understand one's personal relations with one's colleagues, the underlying feelings, and the effects of these on what gets reported is very difficult. It actually requires a second-order analysis, one that is likely to be impossible to do during the field investigation itself. There exist very few accounts of collegial relations and their importance, and these fail for the most part to consider them in the context of scientific objectivity. But one should not mistake the crucial importance of doing so. For anyone who has spent some time sloshing about in the methodological embryo of a research facility at a university, it is crystal-clear that many of the ''empirical observations'' of the real world are hatched here; rationalized accounts of the ''methodological procedures'' used in the collection of research data represent a form of *laundering the data* to hide this truth from us. Just as Nixon's aides laundered the checks through Mexican banks to construct the appearance of a ''rational compliance'' with the election-campaign contribution laws, so do social researchers launder the data to maintain and promote their rational appearances.

During my investigations of social welfare I conceived the influences of one's collegial relations as the problems of the Faust–Mephistopheles dialectic transferred into sociological research. Some of the influences are relatively easy to determine, others more difficult. There is little doubt in my own mind, for example, that the sociological relevance of the topic which I eventually analyzed for the purposes of completing my dissertation—official records and reports—was implicitly suggested to me through the similar interests of two of my mentors, one who had done a previous research investigation of coroner's determinations of suicides and another who was then investigating the official records of drinking drivers. Had it not been for my personal associations with these two men, the relevancies of official records and reports to other theoretical issues in sociology probably would have never occurred to me. Had my dissertation been submitted to a sociology department at a different school, the chances are very great that it wouldn't have been accepted. So that is one influence that seems clear, to me at least. Other influences can be ascertained too. One consequence of my collegial relations is that I brazenly stole some of my colleagues' ideas—for example, in the writing of this chapter. Simultaneously I "loaned" some of mine to them. One mentor referred to this phenomenon as a "symbiotic relationship," jokingly, as he scurried off to publish some of my ideas in one of his papers. I am still thinking about other subtle influences, and this will undoubtedly continue for some time.

One's collegial relations may influence virtually all aspects of any given scientific investigation. The blossoming interest in "the sociology of knowledge" so popular in recent years springs from this insight. John Lofland's observations cited earlier also attest this truth. In Lofland's analyses of the possible factors involved in the decisions to not "tell all" about a research project, we recall, he does not say or suggest that the potential dangers of telling all stem from the members of our local communities, the police, other official control agencies, our families or churches. He emphatically states the withheld information is that which is of a *professionally* discrediting nature. While a literal interpretation of the traditional ethics of scientifically conducted research would lead one to anticipate a stance of "ethical neutrality" by scientists *on methodological issues,* we all know and recognize this stance as a myth. All this urges us to conceive the primordial, gut-level feelings involved in the observer's personal relations with professional colleagues as "feelings about home." We intuitively understand that this is where the heart is, and that the heart has reasons of which reason knows not, as Pascal put it. Using these intuitions often serves us well as a convenient escape from the arduous labors of critical reflection; not to use them is madness.

In several ways the materials presented in this chapter point out the basic conflicts between a substantive and a formal rationality. These conflicts reflect one of the fundamental ambiguities of our Western self-understanding. The profound irony of the sociology of knowledge is that it proposes that we view ourselves as we have traditionally viewed others, the erstwhile subjects of our scientific inquiries and "objects" of our understandings. These "objects" have not been object-like at all, of course, nor are we. The sociology of knowledge always claims for its own questions a privileged exemption from this fact, for the time being at least, and fails to elucidate an understanding of the paradox it is. It hides our natural bonds of community from us, and the ways we know one another as human. Additionally, it fails to enlighten us about the motivational sources of our common interests. This leads to our final consideration.

The Desire

Reflecting for a moment on all we have considered in the last four chapters, including all the problems of gaining entree, developing trusting relations, and evaluating the effects of observation on what is observed, one might wonder why more research projects don't die before completion. Indeed, many do. This fact is not as well appreciated as it deserves to be. We know that many of the graduate students we have known in school say "to hell with it." Even an occasional professor says the same, usually incurring the wrath of his colleagues in the process. The methodological literature contains several references to this kind of going native, perhaps an indication that some find the social realities of those they study a plausible alternative to the social reality of scientific observation.

What distinguishes those who complete a research project from those who do not is very likely a congeries of misadventitious events, circumstantial considerations, and other features of specific situations. This is not a question we need give a great deal of thought. But behind any such trivial distinction lies the natural community of our self-interested curiosities, our passions for a more lucid self-understanding and understanding of others, of how and in what ways the twain meet, or don't. These unite and divide us in everyday life. Very often they are what brought us in hope to the very first sociology class at the university. These passions and curiosities are present whenever we entertain any thoughts of optimism or pessimism, joy or despair. Our feelings of membership in this natural community show themselves by our continued commitments to the institutions of talking and listening, reading and writing, questioning and answering, acting and reflecting. They are most evident when we care so much as to fight bitterly and acrimoniously with one another, when we judge unequivocally and speak in anger. These passionate feelings are only tenuously concealed behind the facades of our words, our "rational accounts." The social reality of word making is the topic of our next chapter.

NOTES

1. William F. Whyte, *Street Corner Society*. Chicago: The University of Chicago Press, 1943, 1955, 288–98.
2. Rosalie H. Wax, "Reciprocity as a Field Technique," *Human Organization*, 11 (1952): 34–7.
3. Donald Roy, "The Study of Southern Labor Union Organizing Campaigns," pp. 216–44 in Robert W. Habenstein, ed., *Pathways to Data*. Chicago: Aldine, 1970, p. 220.
4. Kurt H. Wolff, "Surrender and Community Study," pp. 233–64 in Arthur J. Vidich, Joseph Bensman, and Maurice Stein, eds., *Reflections on Community Studies*. New York: Wiley, 1964.
5. *Ibid.*, p. 256.
6. *Ibid.*, p. 235.
7. *Ibid.*, p. 237.
8. See Blanche Geer, "First Days in the Field," pp. 372–98 in Phillip E. Hammond, ed., *Sociologists at Work*. Garden City, N.Y.: Doubleday, 1964. See also the essays in the volume edited by Habenstein, *op. cit.*
9. This advice is found in several essays in the Habenstein volume and many other essays as well.
10. This is discussed in Alvin W. Gouldner, *The Coming Crisis of Western Sociology*. New York: Basic Books, 1970.

11. One could also speculate that the observer has a weak stomach, and there would be an element of truth to this. On several occasions while visiting friends in hospitals I have passed out, and I have a very deep fear of hospitals.

12. The Foster Home Licensing personnel were continually on the lookout for violations of the official rules on out-of-home care for children. They combed the classified ads in the newspapers daily for people who might be so audacious as to advertise their services. They continually solicited the aid of the social workers in the categorical-aid financial-assistance programs to report any instances of "unofficial placements" or foster care of children. The foster home market wasn't an absolutely monopolized one, but sustained efforts were directed toward making it that way.

13. For a discussion of the relevant literature and research on this see Edwin M. Lemert, "Records in the Juvenile Court," pp. 355–88 in Stanton Wheeler, ed., *On File: Records and Dossiers in American Life*. New York: Russell Sage, 1970.

14. I might add that many of the Child Welfare Services social workers share these sentiments with me, some for entirely different reasons however.

15. For a discussion of the phenomenon of going native, see Benjamin D. Paul, "Interview Techniques and Field Relations," p. 435 in A. L. Kroeber et al., eds., *Anthropology Today*. Chicago: The University of Chicago Press, 1953.

16. The term "natural" is taken from the discussion of the types of informants in field research by John P. Dean, "Participant Observation and Interviewing," pp. 225–52 in John T. Doby, ed., *Introduction to Social Research*. Harrisburg, Pa.: Stackpole, 1954.

17. These references are further elucidated in my "The Social Construction of Official Information," unpublished Ph.D. dissertation, University of California, San Diego, 1973, especially chaps. 3, 7, and 8.

18. In the course of my research a questionnaire distributed to the social workers at Metro by the local Social Services Union said that about one-third of the workers used barbituates during their work activities. I knew there were even several "pushers" in the office, in the sense of persons who kept bottles of phenobarbital in

their desks which others could draw upon as they wished. Personally, I never felt certain that what the questionnaire reported was correct, but there was no apparent reason why anyone would exaggerate about this.

19. To give just one example, at my present place of employment many of my colleagues are unaware of a state statute which specifically proscribes the sexual liaisons of university professors.

20. Colin M. Turnbull, *The Forest People*. New York: Simon & Schuster, 1962.

21. This fact was dramatically emphasized to me through some of the prepublication journal reviews I received when I tried to publish several papers describing the field investigation. In his rejection of one paper, for example, one of the anonymous reviewers for *Social Problems* judged me as having a "perverted sense of morality," and this was the only basis cited for the rejection. One of the few available public accounts of these phenomena is contained in Don Martindale's illuminating discussion of the academic reviews he received about one of his recent analyses. See his "The Mentality of the Crusader," pp. 167–90 in Don Martindale and Edith Martindale, *Psychiatry and the Law*. St. Paul, Minn.: Windflower, 1973.

22. In citing the research literature here, I am specifically indebted to the exceptional analysis by Ned Polsky, "Research Method, Morality, and Criminology," in his *Hustlers, Beats & Others*. Chicago: Aldine, 1967.

23. While I was still in the process of finishing the welfare studies, I became involved with about fifteen of my colleagues in another study where this possibility was a very real one. The study involved the investigation of many different aspects of a national political convention, some of which were covert in nature. Given our understandings about the aftermath of the 1968 Democratic Party Convention in Chicago, we had to consciously come to grips with the nature of our commitments and loyalties at the very beginning and decide what we would do if any of the research information was subsequently the subject of a court subpoena. With relatively few reservations, all of us committed ourselves to "hunkering down" and "stonewalling it" to the end.

24. This reference is specifically to the discussion by Carl B. Klockars of his "research bargains" with professional fences, or receivers of stolen goods. Klockars tells us that the research agreements he worked out with "Vincent" included the understanding that if Klockars were to be hauled into court by a subpoena of his research information, he would reveal his information and sources before going to jail. See his *The Professional Fence*. New York: The Free Press, 1974.

25. John Lofland, *Analyzing Social Settings*. Belmont, Calif.: Wadsworth, 1971, pp. 132–3.

26. The issue is addressed, for instance, by Jack Douglas, "Observing Deviance," pp. 3–33 in Jack D. Douglas, ed., *Research on Deviance*. New York: Random House, 1972.

27. This discussion of the distinction between empathy and sympathy borrows on the analysis of this by Douglas in *ibid*.

28. This advice is found in W. Richard Scott, "Field Methods in the Study of Organizations." Pp. 272–82 in James G. March, ed., *Handbook of Organizations*. Chicago: Rand-McNally, 1962.

29. Peter L. Berger, *The Sacred Canopy*. Garden City, N.Y.: Doubleday, 1967, p. vii.

30. This is a general reference to the personal reflections on scientific careers collected in Irving Louis Horowitz, ed., *Sociological Self-Images,* Beverly Hills, Calif.: Sage, 1970; and the autobiographical interviews contained in many issues of the journal *Issues in Criminology*. In this respect, an especially valuable account is James Watson's story of the events leading to and surrounding the discovery of DNA. See James D. Watson, *The Double Helix*. New York: Signet, 1969.

Chapter 7

Observing, Recording, and Analyzing in Field Research

VARIED MEANINGS attend the words "sociology" and "sociologist." Sociology is commonly linked with social work, socialism, or social reform. From the point of view of a professional practitioner, these traditional connotations are sources of confusion and misunderstanding. But this is a narrow view. The long-standing ambiguities here are more truthfully conceived as expressions of our ongoing struggle to determine the relations between our organized bodies of abstract knowledge and their applications to practical life. Much of the professional folklore in the social sciences is taken up with concerns about the relations between our theoretical interests and practical purposes, such as the realization of socialism, the practice of social work, or the attainment of social reforms. Since these struggles among us are enduring, even necessary and inevitable, we can anticipate that these ambiguities will remain with us for some time.

In reviewing scholarly books and articles of recent years, one is aware that the traditional ambiguities in the meanings of "sociologist" have been supplanted by another meaning in re-

177

cent decades, that of official, in the sense of spy. Evidence for this is found in many writings of those who elucidate their various research problems. The shift in emphasis in meaning reflects an awareness by many members of society of the close relations between the interests of practical sociologists and those of state officials. Materials presented in the previous chapters explicitly and implicitly point out that whatever the abstract definitional distinctions one might wish to make among "sociologist," "researcher," "investigator," "observer," "social scientist," "theorist," and "spy" may be, the meanings of these distinctions are ambiguous for many practical actors in the research settings. During my welfare research, conversational expressions of ambiguity often gave me an opportunity to clarify my understanding of the relations between the practice of sociology and the practical concerns of daily life. In those instances where a relationship of trust had developed, I felt the clarifications were believed. In other instances, no amount of clarification could allay previous doubts and suspicions.

There are other subtleties intertwined with the variable meanings of "sociologist"; the sociologist is commonly considered as one who looks around and takes notes. The motives imputed to one who does this sort of thing run the gamut from pure to venal, from an uncritical imputation that one is bettering mankind to the ironic assertion that a sociologist is one who requires a $10,000 grant to find a whorehouse. Peter Berger's presentation of the sociologist as a Professional Peeping Tom falls somewhere between these extremes:

> We would say then that the sociologist (that is, the one we would really like to invite to our game) is a person intensively, endlessly, shamelessly interested in the doings of men. His natural habitat is all the human gathering places of the world, wherever men come together. The sociologist may be interested in many other things. But his consuming interest remains in the world of men, their institutions, their history, their passions. And since he is interested in men, nothing that men do can be altogether tedious for him. He will naturally be interested in the events that

engage men's ultimate beliefs, their moments of tragedy and grandeur and ecstasy. But he will also be fascinated by the commonplace, the everyday. He may sometimes feel revulsion or contempt. But this also will not deter him from wanting to have his questions answered. The sociologist, in his quest for understanding, moves through the world of men without respect for the usual lines of demarcation. Nobility and degradation, power and obscurity, intelligence and folly—these are equally interesting to him, however unequal they may be in his personal values or tastes. Thus his questions may lead him to all possible levels of society, the best and the least known places, the most respected and the most despised. And, if he is a good sociologist, he will find himself in all these places because his own questions have so taken possession of him that he has little choice but to seek for answers.

It would be possible to say the same things in a lower key. We could say that the sociologist, but for the grace of his academic title, is the man who must listen to gossip despite himself, who is tempted to look through keyholes, to read other people's mail, to open closed cabinets. Before some otherwise unoccupied psychologist sets out now to construct an aptitude test for sociologists on the basis of sublimated voyeurism, let us quickly say that we are speaking merely by way of analogy. Perhaps some little boys consumed with curiosity to watch their maiden aunts in the bathroom later become inveterate sociologists. This is quite uninteresting. What interests us is the curiosity that grips any sociologist in front of a closed door behind which there are human voices. If he is a good sociologist, he will want to open that door, to understand these voices. Behind each closed door he will anticipate some new facet of human life not yet perceived and understood.[1]

As do the previous ideas which liken the sociologist to a seeker of betterment or whorehouses, the metaphor of the Professional Peeping Tom partially distorts actual realities. Some argue that the sociologist's quest for understanding, as Berger calls it, often masks more worldly desires. And there are some who regard professional "voyeurism" as a reflection of complicated historical developments which lead us to the contemporary crises of the impersonal, technological society. They would argue that professional voyeurism is an abrogation of responsibility for a transcendental sociological vision. But on whatever grounds Berger's definition might be faulted, it does include several essential features neglected by previous definitions which depict purity and venality; namely, it says that a sociologist is one who observes, questions, reflects, and makes notes of these activities. In actual sociological practice, such activities are done by those who momentarily absent themselves from cocktail parties to sneak off to the lavatory to make observational notes—to those who sneak off to lavatories to make their observations.[2]

Before the social welfare field research I had completed two minor field investigations. It would appear reasonable to expect one with this experience behind him to be aware of others' definitions of research and researchers. The following notes, made during the third week at Metro, illustrate that this was not so:

> As we were out in the field this afternoon Bill also made some comments about the initial reactions of some of the other social workers to the field research. He said he thought one of the reasons why a couple of the workers remain skeptical about the research involves their observations that I haven't been taking too many notes for the first couple of weeks in the office. One of the others apparently commented that this might mean that I wasn't a researcher after all, but perhaps some sort of spy, just as Frank had speculated at that first meeting. . . . Since I've been carrying a tape-recorder under my jacket all this time, taping most of the conversations and home visits, it never occurred to me that someone could become suspicious because of the failure to take many notes while in the office. Looks like I'm going to have to start playing it more like a "field researcher" from now on, doing those things others expect a field researcher to do when he's doing his thing. I've just realized, after doing field research at Metro for three weeks, I wasn't really doing "normal" field work.

One element of the fundamentally social nature of all research is illustrated in the above excerpt. The field researcher, as any other sociologist, is part and parcel of the setting he seeks to observe and analyze. Furthermore, others make use of this fact to say what seems appropriate for the observer to know. Chapters 4 and 5 in this volume argue that to develop relations of trust is necessary for one to understand this embeddedness of a research project. But the materials in these chapters also show their development is not always a practical possibility. And relations involving trust do not necessarily guarantee the objectivity of the observations. To complicate this complex situation, Chapter 6 shows us how the personal feelings of the observer are mixed into the situation in complex and unstated ways. This chapter examines how a field researcher uses observing, recording, and analyzing to bring some measure of closure to all these ambiguities. The focus is on how one uses whatever devices are available—field notes, tapes, documentary materials, interviews, memory, and so forth—to construct a rational account of social order. The major question of this chapter is how a field investigator acts as an agent of social control to contrive the research eschatology, the social reality of word making. First, however, we will review the traditional methodological literature on this topic.

THE TRADITIONAL CONCEPTIONS OF OBSERVING, RECORDING, AND ANALYZING IN FIELD RESEARCH

All successfully completed researches involve observations and records of observations. With this obvious fact in mind, it is puzzling that there are in the traditional methodological literature so few accounts of how the researcher's observations become transformed into a published document. A few scholars have concerned themselves with this issue; most of these are anthropologists. But even so, there are entire volumes purporting to describe field research which do not mention this.[3]

There is one basic existential fact about observing and recording in sociological field research: a sociologist, like all others, forgets. Therefore, in the observer's efforts to render the research accountable, much would be forgotten or distorted over time without the use of records or other controls for the observations. The important methodological question is, What are the relations between these controls and the intrasubjectivity of the observations?

The traditional methodological writings answer this question by using one of two theories of knowledge. Both are properly called positivistic. Philosophers of science have traditionally termed them the correspondence and coherence theories of truth. Furthermore, both theories are properly termed commonsensical in that they presuppose and take for granted the basic interpretive properties of what Alfred Schutz has analyzed as the natural attitude of daily life. Both theories are grounded in the basic idea that there exists a social world of objective social meanings. These meanings are presumed to be stable and unchanging over time, and known independently of the methods used to understand them.

The correspondence theory of truth was the founding cornerstone of positivism in the social sciences. This theory conceives factual or propositional statements as true if there is an object out there in the world corresponding to the statements. From this perspective, linguistic statements are seen as mirrors or reflections of reality. This theory has for the most part atrophied over time. The primary reason for this is that more and more scholars recognize its inability to come to grips with relational categories, nonmaterial abstractions, and the variable meanings of language itself. However, many theorists still advance this theory. Sociologists Allen Barton and Paul Lazarsfeld write:

> When one examines qualitative reports, one of the first types of material which catches our attention is the "surprising observation." Like the nets of deep-sea explorers, qualitative studies may pull up unexpected and striking things for us to gaze on. We find that there are people who believe that they are being educated by the unrelated and trivial information presented by quiz shows. Interviews with people deprived of their newspaper by a

strike disclose that some do not turn to alternative sources of news, but to reading anything which is lying around the house; a major function of newspaper reading seems to be simply to fill in "gaps" in the daily routine. Observers of the underworld tell us that professional thieves constitute a rather exclusive social group, with exacting standards of membership strongly reminiscent of those of lawful professions. Anthropological data of course are full of surprising observations: that Eskimos lend their wives to guests without any jealousy, that Fiji Islanders kill their chiefs when they grow old, and so on.

These phenomena are of various levels: some are individual beliefs and behaviors, some are a matter of group standards and structures within a society, some involve the norms of a whole culture. In each case the qualitative researcher has simply disclosed that such-and-such a phenomenon exists. And in one way or another, to be told that such things exist has a strong impact on the reader. They all have an element of surprise.[4]

Implicit in this portion of the Barton and Lazarsfeld argument is the idea that the objects studied by the social sciences are essentially equivalent to the objects studied by the natural and physical sciences. Barton and Lazarsfeld even call the objects of social science knowledge "things" in the same vein as Emile Durkheim, in his instruction to view social facts as things. Given this idea, the tasks of the sociological observer's report are to depict their true, objective, factual, real nature. In different terms, the phenomena noted by Barton and Lazarsfeld are seen to "really exist," and the observer's report merely reflects this real, factual existence.

The second positivistic theory of knowledge is the coherence theory of truth. This theory introduces the element of the human knowing mind as the primary component. The real world is thought to be filtered through the mind. This theory receives much greater acceptance and expression than the correspondence theory. The major difference from the correspondence theory is that scientific concepts are now conceived as mental constructs rather than reflections of reality. The coherence theory generally asserts that factual statements are true insofar as they are consistent with the properties of the human knowing mind. Though critical of those who conceive coherence in terms of psychological reductionism, Herbert Blumer promotes a sociological version of this position:

> The position of symbolic interactionism is that the "worlds" that exist for human beings and for their groups are composed of "objects" and that these objects are the product of symbolic interaction. An object is anything that can be indicated, anything that is pointed to or referred to—a cloud, a book, a legislature, a banker, a religious doctrine, a ghost, and so forth. . . . The nature of an object—of any and every object—consists of the meaning that it has for the person for whom it is an object. The meaning sets the way in which he sees the object, the way in which he is prepared to act toward it. An object may have a different meaning for different individuals; a tree will be a different object to a botanist, a lumberman, a poet, and a home gardener; the President of the United States can be a very different object to a devoted member of his political party than to a member of the opposition; the members of an ethnic group may be seen as a different kind of object by members of other groups. The meaning of objects for a person arises fundamentally out of the way they are defined to him by others with whom he interacts. Thus, we come to learn through the indications of others that a chair is a chair, that doctors are a certain kind of professional, that the United States Constitution is a given kind of legal document, and so forth. Out of a process of mutual indications common objects emerge—objects that have the same meaning for a given set of people and are seen in the same manner by them.

Several noteworthy consequences follow from the foregoing discussion of objects. First, it gives us a different picture of the environment or milieu of human beings. From their standpoint the environment consists *only* of the objects that the given human beings recognize and know. The nature of the environment is set by the meaning that the objects composing it have for those human beings. Individuals, also groups, occupying or living in the same spatial location may have, accordingly, very different environments; as we say, people may be living side by side yet be living in different worlds. Indeed, the term "world" is more suitable than the word "environment" to designate the setting, the surroundings, and the texture of things that confront them. It is the world of their objects with which people have to deal and toward which they develop their actions. It follows that in order to understand the action of people it is necessary to identify their world of objects.[5]

The correspondence theory of positivism asserts the existence of one absolutist, physical–material reality from which there are no variations. The coherence theory posits an infinite array of social realities made up of combinations of material objects and individual knowing minds. Despite these differences, however, both express a faith in the existence of an objectively factual social world. This presumption of dualistic independence of the knower from the known is what Husserl, Habermas, and others have called "objectivism." Alvin Gouldner expresses a preference for the label "methodological dualism." [6] By presupposing the factual nature of the social world, scientific investigations done in this vein express their faith in human perception without elucidating the conditions for it, as Maurice Merleau-Ponty has observed.[7]

Presupposing the factual character of the social world leads traditional field researchers in sociology to depict the relations among their observations, recordings, and analyses as having the nature of correspondence,[8] indicators,[9] packaging,[10] coherence,[11] images,[12] representations,[13] comprehensive gross descriptions,[14] and other things.[15] The traditional writings conceive the observational records as a vast technology. There is a voluminous literature on classifications and cross classifications of field notes, types of field notes, and files.[16] The classification schemes assume that research records or controls constitute a language about an independent world of objects. It is a language conceived as truly or falsely connected with those objects independent of an observer's common-sense interpretations and practical situation.

Those advancing the traditional theories of truth have commonly understood these abstract notions as idealizations. If one is realistic about the conduct of science, one would not anticipate their complete realization in actual practice. In reviewing the traditional methodological writings, one learns the traditional practitioners have ways to manage the gap between the ideals and realities, ways which lie beyond the parameters of the theoretical formulation itself. These include appeals to readers to accept the factual claims of the researches on the basis of the professional standing of the claimer,[17] the powerful rhetoric of science,[18] the magic of numbers,[19] the moral omniscience of the observer,[20] or his political sentiments.[21] As readers, we are asked to maintain the "retrospective illusion," as Merleau-Ponty has termed the phenomenon, by writers utilizing the traditional political tools of politicians and parents, power and mystification. The traditional positivistic philosophies of science mentioned in these discussions are, most emphatically, philosophies *for the institutional development of science;* they are not, in any rigorous sense, philosophies *of science.*

The previous chapters suggest we are ill served by maintaining the illusion that the field notes and other observational records kept by an observer during a field project approximate a mirror of reality. These chapters point out that the data collected during an investigation are affected by how the researcher defines the project, how others in the setting define the research, relations of trust, personal feelings, and so forth, and that while some of these may be relatively unproblematic, others are not. Taken together, the discussions bring to mind a sociological counterpart of the Heisenberg uncertainty principle, which recognizes the effect observation has on what is observed in sociological work. This principle alone provides grounds to doubt that a research report is a mirror of reality.

My reflections on my research experiences with observing, note-taking, and analyzing suggest further reason to doubt that research observations simply reflect social reality. When one studies the observational records of research as a topic of interest in and of themselves, they may be seen to consist of a continuous dialectic between substantive and interpretive presuppositions utilized and taken for granted by the observer in order to record notes on the observed phenomena in the first place. In one sense, this affirms the arguments of those who say we are capable of conceptualizing phenomena before we have images of them. Vygotsky, Bruner, and others say this.[22] But there are other important features of the note-taking enterprise which deserve our attention.

An investigator's observational records are highly variable. This fact is supported by many writings in the traditional field-research literature. As a field researcher develops a better understanding of activities in a given setting, the observational records will change to reflect the observer's changing understanding. My field experiences in the social welfare agencies readily support this field-research truth. But there are also other sources of variability. The quantity and quality of the observational records vary with the field worker's feelings of restedness or exhaustion, reactions to particular events, relations with others, consumption of alcoholic beverages, the number of discrete observations, and so forth. Added to these are a wide range of unanticipated technical problems with tape recorders, transcription, and typing and typists; all these seem to continually subvert rational intentions and the best-laid plans.

What is one to make of this combination of the variability of observational records with the previous understandings of the problematics and emergent meanings of field research? Is the point to say that the situational realities of research encroach upon the findings in a seemingly endless number of mis- or nonadventitious ways? This point may be noteworthy, but it is relatively trivial. The more important point to be taken is this: the factual realities reported as findings of a given investigation do not inhere in the research process as such. The factual realities must be organized and put together by the observer. Only the observer's intention to act as an agent of social control provides the apparently rational account of social order. The following materials depict selected features of this process.

USING OBSERVATION, RECORDING, AND ANALYSIS TO CONSTRUCT SOCIAL ORDER

My original research plan involved organizing the data from the social welfare settings with a symbolic interactionist theoretical perspective. Election of this theoretical perspective was justified on traditional grounds. The original proposal referred to the scholarly work of social psychologists and symbolic interactionists in sociology that was responsible for the development of the abstract notions of "group perspectives" and "collective perspectives." The researches and writings of Becker, Geer, Hughes, Suttles, Scott, Blumer, Strauss, and others were cited.[23] Also, several researches of phenomenologists and ethnomethodologists were cited. They were considered as providing creative insights about how members of society produce their daily routines.

These abstract ideas about social order provided a starting point for the inquiry. They did not provide, in any explicit sense, the substantive particulars which seemed to make up the social welfare perspective on social reality. On this score, however, other information was available. Personal acquaintances with social workers and several tape-recorded interviews provided information about some of the major ideas and specialized vocabulary of social workers. For example, one distinction shared among social workers was "being supportive" versus "being punitive." I felt this justified having several anticipations about what would be found in the setting. Namely, there would be a common agreement among the members that their work was related to formally organized sets of rules, but they would accept the possibility of differential interpretations of formal rules. Another early formulation pertained to some of the background meanings considered essential for accomplishing the formal tasks of Child Welfare Services. These included the abstract meanings of normal homes, normal families, normal children, and so forth.

Other than these early formulations, I had only vaguely defined expectations about how I would conduct myself as a field researcher, what would be observed and recorded, etc. The initial research strategy was to "play it by ear." This phrase may have a certain unrigorous sound to it, but it was not factitious. The plan was to pay careful attention to what individuals said to one another, to develop a sensitivity to the nuances of linguistic and paralinguistic communications in the setting, and to take these matters seriously in order to develop a truthful understanding of these actions.

When I began the research at the Lakeside office, my intentions were to return from each day in the field and record "everything that happened." From reading the accounts of the traditional field-research literature, I was already aware this "ideal" was a practical impossibility. I was also aware that several of the seasoned veterans advised against it. However, it was also a common observation that one's ability to record field notes improves with disciplined experience. So I reasoned that any disadvantages resulting from recording everything I could would be offset by the advantages, namely, many data and improved note-taking skills. Thus, during the first week of the research, I spent about nine to ten hours per day in the field plus almost the same amount of time recording field notes. This maddening pace was undoubtedly related to my initial feelings of anxiety. My pace gradually slowed during the project, but for fully eight months of the field observations I saw myself as trying to realize the "ideal" of what Peter Blau terms "the field worker's sixteen hour work day." [24] The illusion that I could do so was maintained in the face of obvious evidence to the contrary and the feelings of guilt which resulted from not making this grade. I finally concluded this "ideal" represents one of many myths of field research practice.

When the research began at Lakeside, there was an official

clearance for tape-recording visits in the homes of welfare clients. The initial plans actually called for the use of two tape recorders. One was a large reel-to-reel recorder carried in a briefcase. It was to be used to record the social worker's comments before and after the home visit. The second (cassette) recorder was small enough to be concealed in my jacket pocket. This one was to be used to record the actual dialogue in the home. On the first home visit of the first day of the research, the social worker refused to allow me in her automobile as long as I carried the large recorder. So the initial plan was discarded in favor of utilizing just the smaller recorder. But cassette recordings existed for only some of the home visits.[25]

When I recorded field notes of the daily observations in the evening, I gave no special status to those interactions recorded on tape. The cassettes of the home visits were not replayed before the field notes were recorded. The major reason for this was the time involved in replaying the cassettes. I tried to record notes on all the visits with accuracy and thoroughness. At the time, this was viewed as a practical strategy to develop note-recording skills. The cassettes of the actual home visits I considered to have a potential for enhancing the master field notes.

As mentioned, the social worker's perspective on social reality was most important at the beginning of the research. My plans called for a careful inspection of the cognitive social rules used by each social worker to organize the activities in a specific case. It was hoped that by recording everything that happened in each CWS case, it would be possible, eventually, to sort out the situationally specific relevancies from the more stable, transsituational elements of what happened. I would then consider these cognitive criteria as constituting the social worker's perspective. I tried to record everything that happened for over five months of the research. I did this in the face of periodic doubts that something was amiss with this course of action. During this time period I was aware my field notes did not in any manner contain a complete, true record of what happened but only a version of some slice of it. The nagging doubt involved a sense that I was trying to do with my field notes precisely what the CWS workers did when they recorded the narrative portion of a welfare case record. Insofar as my note-taking efforts were considered as an attempt to outdo social workers in record keeping, it was painfully obvious my field notes were inferior to the records made by the CWS workers. But the ideal of recording everything that happened was maintained despite the periodic doubts.

Several months passed before I had an opportunity to compare the observations recorded in the field notes with hard evidence, that is, the transcriptions from the cassettes. The reasons for this were financial and technical. First, since the research was not funded, I couldn't afford to have the cassettes immediately transcribed. Second, because of a bizarre technical misalignment problem with one tape recorder, the master field notes for the first six weeks were completely inaudible to the unfamiliar ear of the typist. I had to hand-transcribe these notes, a very slow and tedious process. Thus during the early months I did not have the opportunity for the continuous review of field notes prescribed in the field-research writings.

The eventual comparisons of field notes with transcriptions from the cassettes clarified some of the problems I encountered in the research and some of my nagging doubts. The comparisons also enhanced my understanding of the field-research process.

First, the master field notes reflected an attempt to recapture all the statements of a particular worker as he presented the facts of a case and the diagnosis reached. Grammatical and syntactical structures, as I recalled them, had also been recorded. The transcripts, however, illustrated my illusions. They revealed only my grammar and syntax.

Second, the comparisons indicated that only a relatively small portion of the facts which defined the problem for a family at a specific point in time had been remembered. I initially interpreted this to mean the discovery of the social worker's per-

spective was going to be more difficult than originally anticipated. In fact, the review of materials revealed only one
cognitive criterion definitive of an abnormal home about which I
was certain. Social workers defined a home as abnormal if they
discovered animal or human feces in living and dining areas.
But this applied to a miniscule number of cases. Clear evidence
of systematic child battering appeared to be a widely shared criteria of an abnormal parent. But here there were variations in
what was accepted as clear evidence in a given case, and very
few welfare cases involved child battering. Thus, it seemed as
though the situationally specific facts utilized by a social worker
to define the problems for a family at a specific point in time
were unique for each case. Also, a meaningful fact used by a
social worker to define a client's problem in one case was interpreted differently by other workers for other cases. I felt I
was not making progress toward my goal of elucidating the
social worker's perspective.

Third, comparing notes and cassette transcripts led to an
awareness that features crucial to understanding actions were
not explicitly communicated verbally on many occasions. When
I listened to the cassette recordings of home visits, on several
occasions I realized that I knew certain things about the actions
which had not been stated in so many words. This is not to
imply I had to read between the lines of the transcripts or review
them in an ironic or metaphorical manner to understand them. It
is to say some of the crucial features of the action were not
expressed verbally. Examples of this follow.

In some instances, social workers concealed their intentions
during a home visit in order to pursue them. Thus a worker
would appear interested in understanding the problems of the
family while actually collecting data to be used in a court peti-
tion. Such intentions could not be inferred from the verbal statements in the transcripts. Another example involves the relevance of individual worker's or client's feelings to the
understanding of a given action. Sometimes feelings were expressed at the time of the event, sometimes they were es-

tablished through the worker's later reflections. On some occasions they were not expressed at all. Some were probably inexpressible. This means that many facts which are known to be true are not observable in the strict empiricist sense. For social scientists to retain their empiricist traditions in the face of this obvious truth is to lop off much that is important in everyday life in favor of a commitment to traditional forms.

The comparisons of the field notes with the transcripts of the actual conversations reveal that the observational records of a field-research investigation are inevitably variable. This inevitability results from the natural limitations of an observer's memory, the selectivity of the observer's perception and attention, and the unexpressed nature of many understandings. Originally these factors were seen as possible limitations of the major idea with which I began, that is, that of elucidating the cognitive criteria of the social worker's perspective. At first, I did not see these factors as invalidating the initial idea. Later I did see them thus. Like social workers and other practical investigators, field researchers may virtually ignore information potentially jeopardizing their assumptions.

After months of laborious effort and agonized reflection, there emerged a realization that the conception of a group or collective perspective shared by social workers in general, though justified on high authority by the traditions of sociology, had been maintained at the expense of maintaining the integrity of the individual social workers' socially meaningful experiences. This realization was not experienced as a turning point. There was no specific moment when the anomalies revealed their previously obscure meanings and generated insights of a higher truth. The process was not that rational in its development. Rather, by using an empathetic understanding of the events at the office and the workers involved in them, I was led to *seek out* different analytical conceptions which more truthfully retained the integrity of the social workers' experiences.

Even though there was not a specific turning point in the field observations, one series of events appears, in retrospect, very crucial for my empathetic understanding. It involved a relatively minor happening in the setting, but it was important because it afforded new insights for me. In abstract terms, it stimulated my thinking about the workers' different substantive interpretations of what one might otherwise think of as the same event. The ideas I got led eventually to a rethinking about the nature of the official record-making processes. The events involved the CWS workers' completion of a report called the Annual Time Study. This was one of many documentary and statistical reports done by the workers as a routine part of their tasks. This particular report was seen by the CWS workers to possess actual or potential political meanings. After the report was completed and submitted, it was "kicked back" by higher administrative authorities, who expressed a desire for a recomputation of its statistics. The same thing occurred two more times after that.[26] While further details of the event will not be presented at this point, the following excerpt from the field notes depicts some of my thoughts on it:

> Would like to add some thoughts . . . regarding the Time Study. For the most part it still appears as though I understand little about how the social workers make the agency work. It's truly ironic that I should record a field note after my very first day of research at Lakeside to the effect that I really had a feeling for what Schutz was saying when he said that he had at least asked the relevant questions. Now, after nearly eight months in the field, and almost six at Metro, I'm less than certain that Schutz is deserving of all the hero worship he has received. But for some reason, and I don't know why, I really feel that I "got inside" on that Time Study [a reference to the expressed concern of several scholars for "seeing society from the inside"], I feel certain that I understand the thing, largely due to fortuitous circumstances providing the opportunity to be sure. I even feel that I know more about these events than virtually anyone else down there [at the office], and I'm certain that's the case with respect to many of the social workers. On the one hand, I've seen Frank and Betty accomplish the Time Study by using basically the same procedures, yet their experiences of the events were reported very differently.

On the other hand, Frank and Bill used different methods, but talked of their experiences in essentially the same terms. Now I know well that any abstract analytic conception I use to describe the Time Study implying that all of the social workers shared either the same operational methods of doing the report or the same experiences of the events will necessarily destroy part of the truth of this matter. And there's another feature of this Time Study which keeps gnawing at me too, and I really don't know how to deal with this because it's difficult to compare what occurred here with many of the other activities. While my observations at Metro thus far lead me to think Schutz was 99% correct in arguing that the practical actor suspends his doubt rather than his belief in the objects of the so-called "outer world," some of the comments Frank made to me as he was completing the third version of the report don't fit into this neat dichotomy. As he told me what he was doing, he compared this to what Nancy had done, and noted there were distinctively different ways of handling this matter. But then, he further observed that both ways yielded results equally as true, equally as accurate, even though the report didn't call for just an estimate or range, or as Bill sometimes puts it, a "ballpark figure." According to Frank's comments, he wasn't saying that the actual numbers were relative, but that the different ways of conceiving the task were relative; that Nancy had conceived the task differently, but this conception was also a quote true unquote one. In one sense this isn't anything new. Buzz, Metro's Dostoevskian philosopher-in-residence, makes comments nearly every morning he entertains his students in the coffee room to the effect that it is his belief rather than his doubt which he is suspending. But these are typically abstract statements, removed from the context of accomplishing any practical task, and I suspect everyone there in the coffee room sees them in such [an abstract] vein. Frank's comments, on the other hand, are the first examples of this suspension within the context of actually doing some task-at-hand. Still not certain what to make of all this.

The events related to the completion of the Annual Time Study did not produce immediate changes in my thinking. Eventually, however, I reached this conclusion: though I thought I had taken the social workers' activities seriously, it appeared I had had an implicit assumption from the beginning of the research that these activities were really epiphenomenal to some underlying collective perspective on social welfare. What I had observed while doing observation and what I accorded the status of data for the project, then, were partially determined by the *conclusions* with which the research began.

Other unrelated and discontinuous events occurred in the middle months of the research which enabled me to understand that there was not a set of universally shared rational criteria defining the social worker's perspective on reality. This is not to say there was no special common knowledge among social workers. It is not to say they acted irrationally. It is not to say their world was a do-your-own-thing world. It is to say the meanings of welfare membership were variable. Workers were variously seen by others, and saw themselves, as supportive, punitive, conservative, liberal, client advocates, milquetoasts, and so on. More importantly, these distinctions made significant differences in what got done to or with welfare clients. This emphasizes the emergent, problematic, creative, and entrepreneurial aspects of some of the welfare activities.

Many examples of the above points could be given. One concerns a worker's decision about whether or not a foster-home placement is warranted in a given case. On many occasions, a decision for foster-home placement was subject to practical constraints. If there were no available foster homes, a worker's judgment was not realized in practice. These organizational practicalities were not one of the givens of the situation, however. The practical constraints were periodically transcended by a worker's ingenuity and enterprise in creating a new foster home from available resources. Such activities were not isolated; on the basis of the most reliable information, nearly one-half of the foster-home placements made during the year of the research observations were made in homes that were not officially foster homes.

Awareness of such facts emerged only after I began to view my original assumptions about the collective perspective as problematic. Once this occurred, my attention refocused on how the situations themselves were defined. Gradually I began to "hear different things said" in the setting. This happened through a shift in attention from what was said or done to how it was said or done. The following excerpts from the field notes illustrate several instances of my changing awareness. From the notes near the end of the sixth month of the observations:

> Another thing that happened today. I was standing by Bill's desk when Art passed by and asked Bill to cover the phone for a couple of minutes while he walked through a request for County Supp over to Bess Lanston, an EW supervisor. Now I don't know how many times I've heard a comment like that; so many times that it's not even problematic any more. In fact, it's so routine that I'm surprised that I even made any note to remember it. The striking feature about this is that in my first days at Metro I would have wanted to know all about what kind of form he was taking over there, what County Supp was, why and how one used it, got it, didn't get it, or whatever, who and where Bess Lanston was, what she did and so on. But all the time I've missed what was crucial about such a comment, the fact that he was *walking it through*. Before I would have only heard what he was doing or why, but today, instead, I began to hear the *how*.

The notes four days later record this:

> I listened to Michelle's interview with Greta again last night, the one on doing the records and statistics. I've listened to that tape six or eight times, although not for six months or so, and tonight was the first time I actually heard Greta use the phrase "building a case," which really seems fantastic, because she must have used that phrase twenty times within the space of ten minutes.

From the notes at the beginning of the seventh month of field investigations at the Metro office:

> I spent all of the afternoon with Irv today as he was on intake. He made a comment that made me feel like the colossal idiot. He was telling me about his recent investigation of an alleged child-beating, case name of Blauner I think. After he told me how he

happened to get the case and where the call had originated, he said he went to the home to investigate. He said he could tell the mother didn't intend the bruises because of the way they were situated. How many times in the past would I have followed a statement like this with a question about how they were situated? Is it actually possible I could have been doing field research for over six months at Metro without investigating *intention?* This is especially strange because of all the reading I've done about this. It's so obvious now that I've said it that it's embarrassing to record a note on it. What was it [another field researcher] said about chagrin? My research hasn't started yet!

The excerpts from the field notes presented here are necessarily very truncated accounts of the complicated research processes of observation and data collection, but they do illustrate some of the important developments in the research. Taken together, they point out one of the crucial features of sociological research. There is no direct, one-to-one relationship between a field worker's observations and what are recorded as data for the research. Data collection does not reflect what is observed as such. Rather, what an observer collects as data is dependent on what he defines as relevant. Whether preconceived or developed from the ongoing observations, the researcher's categories of relevance determine what he will see as data when doing observation.

While (as previously noted) my initial ideas about the collective perspective of social workers served to constrain the field observations to some extent, I also recorded notes on many topics not directly related to the daily encounters between social workers and welfare clients. My files, coding systems, tapes, and cross classifications of these topics became so complicated that before long I developed a "master coding system" which indicated only the location or nature of my other classification schemes and notes. Within a short time the materials I had collected, including documents, official records, written and tape-recorded observational notes, tape-recorded home visits and interviews, and analytical outlines and notes became so massive that my next several years were a round of "forgetting" and "rediscovering" them.

After about two months at Metro, I began to have a greater appreciation of the relevance of all the official records and reports to the social workers. These records and reports were not only relevant because their completion involved the expenditure of much time and effort, but also because their completion was often related to what a given social worker did, planned, or avoided in a particular welfare case. Having concluded that I would have to "master" these recording and reporting procedures in order to understand their relevance to other actions, I devoted considerable time and effort during the early months to understand how all these records and reports were constructed and used. I kept an ongoing descriptive outline of the important considerations essential for completing each of the major records and reports and, additionally, an analytical outline of my more abstract or theoretical ideas about what was going on. At about the sixth month of my stay at Metro I dictated a rough draft of these descriptions and analyses which resulted, after transcription, in about 100 single-spaced pages. I remember that at the time I saw myself as "getting this out of the way" so that I could continue with my investigation of social casework practice. As it turned out, these 100 pages became the rough draft of my dissertation, *The Social Construction of Official Information,* which was one of two volumes wherein I reported the research observations—along with my unpublished *Doing Social Casework.*

My approach to writing the first draft of the field observations and analyses was varied. Some portions were only descriptive in nature, with little analysis on my part; other materials were organized along the lines of the analytical ideas I held at that time. Still others either described or analyzed a "natural history" or sequence of specific events. In each and every case, however, I found the rough drafts of the chapters lacking. My initial review of the rough draft stimulated many thoughts about what additional observational data should be collected, lines of questioning to be pursued, interviews to be conducted, documents to be collected, and so forth. The first draft was so "rough," in fact, and contained so many holes and gaps of various kinds, that I concluded that writing the first draft of the research report prior to leaving the research settings is an absolutely crucial part of a field-research project.

The point was made earlier that it is a mistake to view the observational records of a research project as merely "reporting" or "reflecting" the factual realities with which the author is concerned. This point also applies to the research report(s), the "final product" of the investigation. Writing the research report(s) not only reflects the author's thinking at a given point in time but also serves as a stimulus for further thought and reflection. This writing process will, at the least, possibly result in several different "stories," as Fred Davis has called them.[27] When guided by the intention to build progressively more theoretical analyses which still retain the actor's perspective, however, hopefully the end result of this writing–reflection process will be a view (or views) which progressively illuminate(s) and encompass(es) the previous one.

CONCLUDING REMARKS

Previous chapters document the importance of relations of trust in field research. The discussions in them show that what an observer will be allowed to see in the setting and what one will be told about the activities there will vary according to the existing relations of trust. These are seldom unproblematic, largely because of the existence of a sociological equivalent of the Heisenberg uncertainty principle, or the effects of observation on what is observed. The important result of this is that a field researcher engages in a continuous and self-organizing process of evaluating the adequacy, validity, and reliability of the research information. Many rules of thumb are employed by field researchers to do these evaluations. Many are situationally and personally specific. All are of a commonsensical nature. But the previous chapters also point out that these efforts produce mixed results. In some instances it is possible to tell how and in what way the observer affected the situation. In others it is more difficult. In many, however, there are no existent criteria for making an evaluation one way or the other. An irreducible element of mystery remains a part of all research.

This chapter documents some of the problematics of observation, recording, and analysis in field research. Some of the conditions affecting the investigator's recording of the field observations are noted. The important point is that what an investigator collects as data for the research is dependent on his presuppositions and categories of relevance. These presuppositions include taken-for-granted notions about the nature of human perception, of language, and of practical reasoning, substantive ideas about the observed actions, and so forth.

In the traditional field-research literature there are several instances where it is plausible to infer that the conclusions of the research were largely determined prior to the collection of data.[28] One account explicitly states that the researcher instructed the members of the setting about what she wanted to find out from them.[29] Because of the great amount of time and effort which go into a field-research investigation, it is always to be hoped that this not occur. This possibility, however, is not guaranteed by the practice of field research.

The materials presented in this chapter illustrate in several ways how an observer achieves a progressive realization of the presupposed notions of the project. They show how some important ideas emerge and change over time, how an observer strives for a more objective, or intersubjective, understanding of the social realities observed. Despite this striving, what one reports as the research findings still is not inherent in the observations or field notes as such, nor does a disciplined awareness of the subtleties of the research process set all things straight.

Even if one has conducted a field-research investigation in the most heroic and conscientious fashion imaginable, one's understandings still have to be put together in a coherent manner. How this mysterious synthesis is accomplished depends, at least in part, on one's purposes.

With respect to the social welfare investigation which concerns us throughout this volume, it was my intention to provide detailed ethnographic descriptions of the substantive realities in the setting. Furthermore, I intended to use these materials to develop a theoretical understanding of these realities. My intentions reflect a choice as to relevance. What gets put together during an enterprise and how it is put together are determined by such decisions.

There are two important implications of this. First, the observer's decisions mean that many of the features constituting the project will be presupposed, taken for granted, and not accorded status as topics for analysis. Second, decisions about the scope of the substantive materials reported mean that less will be described in a literal sense than is supposedly required in science. Much will be depicted synecdochically, glossed, and represented. Presentations of data in the research report, no matter how conscientiously collected or reported, still do not reflect the factual realities of the observations in an absolute sense. They illustrate the field researcher's performance as an agent of social control and the empathetic understandings achieved during the research. This means that any particular research report will provide a reader with various possibilities for criticism, denigration, or ironic comparison.

NOTES

1. Peter L. Berger, *Invitation to Sociology*. Garden City, N.Y.: Doubleday, 1963, pp. 18–9.
2. These contrasts are taken from the researches reported by David Riesman and Jeanne Watson, "The Sociability Project: A Chroni-

cle of Frustration and Achievement," pp. 270–371 in Phillip E. Hammond, ed., *Sociologists at Work,* Garden City, N.Y.: Doubleday, 1964; and Laud Humphreys, *Tearoom Trade,* Chicago: Aldine, 1970.

3. One of the few sociologists addressing this issue is Kurt H. Wolff in his "The Collection and Organization of Field Materials: A Research Report," pp. 240–54 in R. N. Adams and J. J. Preiss, eds., *Human Organization Research: Field Relations and Techniques.* Homewood, Ill.: Dorsey, 1960. Wolff's discussion includes other references existing in the anthropological literature.

4. Allen H. Barton and Paul F. Lazarsfeld, "Some Functions of Qualitative Analysis in Social Research," pp. 163–96 in George J. McCall and J. L. Simmons, eds., *Issues in Participant Observation.* Reading, Mass.: Addison-Wesley, 1969, p. 165.

5. Herbert Blumer, *Symbolic Interactionism.* Englewood Cliffs, N.J.: Prentice-Hall, 1969, pp. 10–1.

6. Alvin W. Gouldner, *The Coming Crisis of Western Sociology.* New York: Basic Books, 1970.

7. Maurice Merleau-Ponty, *The Visible and the Invisible.* Translated by Alphonso Lingis and edited by Claude Lefort. Evanston, Ill.: Northwestern University Press, 1968, pp. 14–49.

8. See Arthur J. Vidich and Gilbert Shapiro, "A Comparison of Participant Observation and Survey Data," *American Sociological Review,* 20 (1955): 28–33.

9. See Howard S. Becker, "Problems of Inference and Proof in Participant Observation," *American Sociological Review,* 23 (1958): 652–60.

10. See Leonard Schatzman and Anselm L. Strauss, *Social Research in the Field: Strategies for a Natural Sociology.* Englewood Cliffs, N.J.: Prentice–Hall, 1973.

11. John F. Lofland, *Analyzing Social Settings.* Belmont, Calif.: Wadsworth, 1971.

12. Blumer, *op. cit.*

13. See Schatzman and Strauss, *op. cit.*

14. See Donald Roy, "Southern Labor Union Organizing Campaigns," pp. 216–44 in Robert W. Habenstein, ed., *Pathways to Data.* Chicago: Aldine, 1970.

15. For a representative sampling of the varied conceptions of these relations, see the thirteen essays in the volume edited by Habenstein, *op. cit.*

16. Discussions of such classifications may be found in the following works: Peter M. Blau, *The Dynamics of Bureaucracy,* Chicago: The University of Chicago Press, 1963, pp. 269–305; Blanche Geer, "First Days in the Field," pp. 272–98 in Phillip E. Hammond, ed., *Sociologists at Work,* Garden City, N.Y.: Doubleday, 1964; Lofland, *op. cit.;* Stephen A. Richardson, "A Framework for Reporting Field Relations Experiences," *Human Organization,* 12, 3 (Sept. 1953): 31–37; William F. Whyte, *Street Corner Society,* 2d ed., Chicago: The University of Chicago Press, 1955. Other discussions may be found in several of the papers in the volume edited by Adams and Preiss, *op. cit.*

17. See, for example, Barney G. Glaser and Anselm L. Strauss, *The Discovery of Grounded Theory.* Chicago: Aldine, 1967, pp. 8–9.

18. Variations of this theme are found in many works, for example, Whyte, *op. cit.;* Blau, *op. cit.;* and several of the essays in Habenstein, ed., *op. cit.*

19. One example of this is Howard Becker's rhetorical reference to the fact that the research files "contain approximately five-thousand single-spaced pages." See Becker, *op. cit.:* 653. Being fair to Becker, however, requires one to mention the existence of many variations of this usage by many others.

20. One of the more interesting commentaries on the morality of participant observation is that of Herbert J. Gans. According to Gans's argument, participant observation is a form of "psychological espionage," a participant observer "has no other choice" than to deceive people, and, furthermore, "often the only way to get honest data is to be dishonest in getting it." See Herbert J. Gans, "The Participant Observer as a Human Being: Observations on the Personal Aspects of Field Work," pp. 300–17 in Howard S. Becker, Blanche Geer, David Riesman, and Robert S. Weiss, eds., *Institutions and the Person: Essays Presented to Everett C. Hughes.* Chicago: Aldine, 1968. The observations presented here are taken from p. 314. It is entirely possible that arguments similar to those made by Gans stimulated Edward Shils's judgment that participant observation represents a "mor-

ally obnoxious . . . form of manipulation,'' although such a judgment could just as likely stem from Shils's methodological Puritanism. See Edward A. Shils, "The Calling of Sociology," pp. 1405–48 in Talcott Parsons et al., eds., *Theories of Society*. New York: The Free Press of Glencoe, 1961.

21. There has been much abstract discussion about the relations between political sentiments and the conduct of sociological research, but very few data which describe the exact nature of the relations. A penetrating critique of various field researches carried out by labeling theorists in sociology as related to this issue is Alvin W. Gouldner's "The Sociologist as Partisan: Sociology and the Welfare State," *The American Sociologist,* 3 (May 1968): 103–16. One of the more interesting commentaries tending to support Gouldner's arguments is that of David Matza. Seven years after the publication of his award-winning *Delinquency & Drift,* Matza tells us, "The entire book is an attack on the juvenile court." With respect to his other scholarly works, Matza observes, "Oh, Wow! Let me preface this by saying *Delinquency & Drift* and *Becoming Deviant* reflected the way I thought at a certain time. I don't think exactly that way right now." These statements are taken from pp. 50 and 48 respectively of an interview conducted by Joseph G. Weis in September 1970 and published as "Dialogue with David Matza," *Issues in Criminology,* 6, 1 (Winter 1971): 33–53.

22. See L. S. Vygotsky, *Thought and Language,* Cambridge, Mass.: M.I.T., 1962; and Jerome S. Bruner et al., *A Study of Thinking,* New York: Wiley, 1956.

23. The general idea of "collective perspectives" is developed either explicitly or implicitly in many of the works of the symbolic interactionists in sociology. The conception is explicitly developed by Howard S. Becker, Blanche Geer, and Everett C. Hughes in their *Boys in White: Student Culture in Medical School,* Chicago: University of Chicago Press, 1961, and their *Making the Grade,* New York: John Wiley, 1968. Also see Blanche Geer, *op. cit.;* and her "Studying a College," in Habenstein, ed., *op. cit.*

24. Blau, *op. cit.,* pp. 269–86.

25. The smaller tape recorder was used for all the research observations conducted at the three offices in Northern Metropolitan

County at the beginning of the project, and for approximately the first three to four months of the observations at the Metro office in Southern Metropolitan County. Use of the recorder was discontinued at this point, to a large extent because it was judged to be less effective than originally anticipated. As the following materials of this chapter explain in greater detail, things that some came to realize crucial for an understanding of what was taking place during a home visit were not formulated as explicit verbal statements during the home visit itself.

26. A more detailed account of these events may be found in chap. 8, "Manipulating Official Statistics: The Case of The Annual Time Study," pp. 359–415 in my "The Social Construction of Official Information," unpublished Ph.D. dissertation, Department of Sociology, University of California, San Diego, 1973.

27. See Fred Davis, "Stories and Sociology," *Urban Life and Culture,* 3, 3 (October 1974): 310–17.

28. See note 22.

29. See Rosalie H. Wax, *Doing Field Work.* Chicago: The University of Chicago Press, 1971, p. 79.

Chapter 8

Reconsidering Objectivity in Sociology

THE FIRST CHAPTER noted the resurgence of interest in participant observation and field research in sociology. This resurgence is intertwined with the philosophical, theoretical, and methodological debates of the current objectivity crisis in the social sciences. It is also tied in with several of the programs proposed as alternatives to the traditional view of scientific conduct, that of positivist objectivism.

Positivist objectivism provided a model of normative ideals which scientists utilized for accepting propositional statements into an organized body of knowledge or rejecting them. At the philosophical level, this model intended a categorical separation between the knowing subject and the objects of knowledge. This is commonly termed subject–object dualism. Two cognitive criteria were considered fundamental for the model, controlled observation and independent verification of the observational realities. Given a sincere application of the substantive specifics of these two general rules, the knowledge obtained from observational inquiry was considered to be actually or potentially free of any subjective, personal, or common-sense elements. The rules of verification themselves were accorded an absolute status; they never had to be tested against anything else, such as some broader notion of human utility.

The first chapter also presented details of the many scholarly writings which are in one way or another concerned with the current objectivity crisis. The diversity of these arguments must be emphasized. They originate from several intellectual disciplines and do not constitute any unified whole. These scholarly contributions reflect a fundamental challenge to the traditional conception of social science objectivity. One of the major points made in many of these works of intellectual self-criticism is that the world of "natural facts" with which positivism concerns itself reflects a metaphysical presupposition about the nature of being in general. Thus, this factual world is not "discovered" by science, but depends on a philosophical justification for its intelligibility. The major implication of this is that, instead of being founded on intersubjective cognitive criteria, the objectivity of the objectivist model is dependent on the common-sense meanings of membership in the scientific language community. This suggests the possibility that what passes as scientific truth for some may bear little relationship to the empirical realities of daily life. On this point Egon Bittner writes:

> For in all the technicality, precision, and formalism that attached to positivist methodology, the object of its objectivity vanished. That is, the suspicion is stirring that it is not only farfetched to expect that a prestige scale might measure prestige in the way the notion is conceived theoretically, but it seems likely that it does not measure anything at all! [1]

Several alternatives to the previous objectivist models have been proposed during the last decade. These alternative formulations are also very diverse. With some qualifications, they share a common rejection of the categorical and oversimplified subject–object dualism of the positivist philosophical commitments. All share a common recognition of the complicated, if as yet unarticulated, interdependences between the knowing subject and the objects of knowledge. What has become less and less plausible to more and more social scientists in recent years, then, is the absolutist conception of objectivity predicated on this subject–object dualism. At one time it might have been plausible to think that the actions of members of society were "objectively determined" by their social situations and practical involvements while scientists viewed these actions from a privileged position of relative detachment or else "floated free" from this daily flux. But it is exceptionally difficult to hang on to such a thought in good faith today, especially when it is so obvious that scientists are increasingly involved in the practical problems of society.

The proposed alternatives to positivist objectivism also put forth a new conception of objectivity for the social sciences, although this is left implicit in some writings. This emerging conception of objectivity has been articulated in various ways; writings speak of maintaining the integrity of the phenomenon, remaining faithful to the phenomenon, retaining the integrity of the phenomenon, and so forth. Put differently, the proposed alternatives put forth a different conception of "the phenomenon" to be studied by the social sciences, and this is related to the different conception of objectivity. Even though there have been modifications of the positivist approaches during this century, throughout all these the instruction has been to conceive the primordial phenomenon of the social sciences to be man as an object, in principle no different from the objects studied by the natural and physical sciences. For positivism, knowledge was to be considered objective to the extent that its production approximated the normative conventions of the natural and physical sciences. All the alternative views share a common recognition of the distinctive nature of the phenomenon to be studied by the social sciences. While there are some differences, all the alternatives generally conceive man as an active subject, one who is actually or potentially capable of exercising choices and assuming responsibility for their consequences. The crucial reference point is one of social individuals who intentionally organize the meaningfulness or meaninglessness of their lives. Along with this generally shared idea about the fundamental phenomenon appropriate for the studies of the social sciences, the alternative proposals to positivism express an interest in understanding how social meanings are constructed in actual settings, and how these constructions are constrained by the cultures, societies, and other expressions of power in which they are embedded. From this view, objectivity is not a matter of assessing the technical adequacy of claims to knowledge, but a matter of assessing their substantive validity. Readers or hearers are asked to evaluate the objectivity of a claim to knowledge according to their reflexive self-related understandings of the basic features of social interaction and human communications as well as their common-sense knowledge of cultural meanings. The positivist approaches promoted a normative conception of objectivity; the alternatives suggest an interpretive one.

It is very uncertain whether the proposed alternatives to scientific positivism will succeed in developing a more truthful self-understanding. Emile Durkheim's instruction to "regard social facts as things" proved to be a slogan without substance, and this may be the fortune of "maintaining the integrity of the phenomenon." Even if the alternatives are successful, however, the relationship between this goal of a reflexive self-understanding and the practical realization of our transcendental visions of a brighter future is even more uncertain.

If there is to be substance to the new promise, participant-observational field research will play an increasingly important role. This is not to deny the legitimacy of other forms of participant observation. For example, I for one consider it thoroughly legitimate to investigate the basic physiological properties of the human body. In this type of research, as in other investigations of nonmeaningful behaviors, there is every reason to think that, while the inquiries would obviously be grounded in common-sense perceptions, the observer effects on the observations would be relatively minimal. Experimental participant observation is unquestionably superior to field research for this and similar problems. The promise of field research is unique in one respect, however. It promises a theoretical understanding of socially meaningful activities as experienced by the members of society, at least insofar as this is possible. It promises an understanding grounded in the actual realities of daily life rather than one which reflects the observer's perceptual faith or the realities of an academic subculture. But this remains a promise. Sufficient evidence already exists to serve as a warning against confusing the product with the promise. The conflicting field researches about Tepoztlan reported by Lewis and Redfield are a classic example.[2] And there are more recent ones too. Nearly a decade after the publication of his award-winning *Delinquency & Drift,* for instance, David Matza's reflections instruct us to view the entire effort as epiphenomenal to his political sentiments at the time.[3] Field research has the potential to generate knowledge based on intersubjective cognitive criteria, but field-research practice does not guarantee that this will result.

On several occasions in this book a contrast has been drawn between the positivist traditions and the emerging alternatives. This contrast might give one the impression that the problems of social science objectivity may be solved by making some kind of "existential choice" between the two. The major thrust of all the preceeding chapters is that this is not so. Few of the problems of developing an intersubjective understanding are solved by making a glib choice about one's loyalty to the phenomenon of the inquiry. Most of the previous chapters reflect this crucial reality. An observer's theoretical orientations and other value commitments are of some importance, but these are not the realities of primary importance for the research. An observer's abstract thoughts do not in any definitive way solve the problems which result from the fact that he is personally involved in and partially constitutes the settings he seeks to observe, record, understand, and analyze. An example from the previous chapter will clarify this point. I mentioned that I began the field-research project on welfare activities intending to organize the observational data with a symbolic interactionist perspective, or, more specifically, with the symbolic interactionist ideas about group or collective perspectives. I felt this choice to be justified on the grounds of accredited sociological tradition. The chapter included materials to show that this choice exercised a considerable influence on the observations for many months. That is, my personal commitment to the traditional theoretical forms influenced what was accorded the status of observational data. One of the major points of Chapter 7 was to show how my ideas changed over time. By contrast, however, the original choice of theoretical perspective had little relationship to how I actually conducted myself as an observer during the project. And yet it was precisely this research conduct, as well as how others in the setting defined it, which was so crucial for the subsequent assessments of the validity of the observational data.

Several of the previous chapters have stressed the problematic and emergent nature of field-research events. The important implication of this is that how an observer becomes personally involved in the events is related to the kind of information he receives. In Chapter 3, for example, it was mentioned that the major reason why the problems of gaining and managing entree are so important is that their resolution will affect how the observer will be socially defined in the setting. This, in turn, is related to what an observer will be allowed to see and what the members will tell him about their activities. In this light, entree is not something that is relevant only to the beginning stages of the research. Its relevance affects the factual realities of the observations. It is necessary to understand the members' various interpretations of the entree situation in order to evaluate the observational data. Chapter 4 supported the arguments advanced by many others in the traditional field-research literature about the essential importance of personal relations of trust. Again, the importance of this does not result from the fact that developing trust represents but one of several different methodological techniques of field research. Developing trust is important because how it is done affects the observational data. Much of the traditional field-research literature about trust implies that its accomplishment is largely impersonal, that is, technical in nature. Chapter 4 advanced several exceptions to this implication. The argument was that field research is necessarily and inevitably personal in several important respects. But this is *not* to say that field research is *completely* personal in nature. Sociologists Richard Berk and Joseph Adams apparently think that field research is a completely personal matter when they write that "good participant observers . . . are born and not made." [4] I do not agree with this. While I think there is an irreducible personal element in all research, I believe that many features of the research process are transpersonal and transsituational. This belief is expressed in all the previous chapters. While taking exception to the arguments of the traditional literature on some points, in each chapter I affirmed some of the cultural wisdom found in the traditional writings. We will clearly understand much more about the degree and extent to which research involves personal elements if sociologists pay much greater attention to the research process as a topic of investigation in itself.

Chapter 5 detailed some of the problematic features of personal relations in field research. The argument was made that despite the "good intentions" of the observer, his actual practices may produce mixed results. After reflecting on this for some time, I think this should be anticipated for all settings which involve morally pluralistic realities. This clearly includes most public settings in American life. This anticipation would also apply to distinctive groups such as sectarian religious movements.[5] The implications of this are clear: it is incumbent on a field researcher to use his sociological competencies to evaluate the research process itself. I mentioned in Chapter 5, for example, that it was my evaluation that my field observations of the welfare activities were characterized by a routinization bias and a public-morality bias. I believe our understandings of social research could be enhanced to some small extent by greater candor about the limitations of our observations. Greater candor won't set all things right, but it might help.

Chapter 6 mentioned the various ways an observer's personal feelings become fused with the rational cognitions represented in his final report. It is clear that some of these are relatively unimportant. Others, however, are fundamental determinants of the entire project. Several instances where an observer's feelings of loyalty or membership became basic determinants of the research observations have been cited in previous pages. Assessing such possible influences requires a measure of self-understanding. This is not so much to emphasize the importance of private introspection as it is to emphasize that of self-observation.[6] The two are clearly not the same. I am personally convinced, for example, that most individuals are very selective about what they see of their own activities, and there are certainly some very pragmatic motives for this. On the basis of my experiences recording observations and my notes on my actual field-research conduct during the social welfare investigation, I am equally convinced that this applies to me as well. If I had not actually studied the research process during the investigation itself, and instead had produced a retrospective account of how the research was accomplished, I am quite sure that I would have produced an idealized and overrationalized account of the research very similar to many which now exist. This is largely why I have tried to resist the temptation to mythologize the research experiences by translating them into the language of "ethical problems."

In Chapter 7, the point was taken that even when an observer is consciously motivated to achieve some authentic approximation of the traditional scientific ideal of literal description, this is impossible. There are several reasons for this. First, in any particular empirical inquiry it is necessary and inevitable that an observer will take much for granted and leave much at a common-sense level of discourse. This does not involve presuppositions in the conventional technical sense of simply forgetting to state some tacit position one holds. But it does involve presuppositions in the philosophical sense of making assumptions about the conditions of possibility.[7] Second, what will be selected out and reported is dependent on the observer's purposes and the intended or solicited audience of the communication. Given my substantive interests in welfare activities (and even field research), there is for me a certain sense of necessity or inevitability concerning what was reported; what was reported as factual reality seemed to flow quite naturally. Furthermore, it is easy to see how the same observational materials could have been used by someone else for an entirely different research investigation.

When we understand that literal description is impossible and that it is necessary for the observer to select out those features of the research that are in accord with his categories of relevance, the research report cannot be judiciously seen as meeting the criteria of clear persuasive intent definitive of the classical notion of rhetoric. Yet the descriptions of the observational realities may be conceived as rhetorical in a much broader sense. This is not, most emphatically, to say the accounts are political or partisan in any *specific* sense. It is to point out that in intending to reach an audience, the communicator undertakes a certain kind of human caring for "the other." Concerning this human caring, there is certainly no ontological necessity which determines that our writing, speaking, reading, or hearing will be ineluctably driven toward some vaguely defined goal of absolute rational clarification. Our personal commitments to the social institutions of communication and silence are perhaps just as often motivated by desire to be accepted by others, to elaborate what we already believed to be true, to support our personal sense of the real, and so forth. It is this very serious human caring for one another which is the crux of the matter. Nowhere is this more evident than when we reflect on the nature of our personal involvements in political affairs, whether those of the party, office, factory, or family. Not long ago Murray Kempton wrote:

> I think there is a change now in our view of life; we know more than we ever knew before, but we know it instinctively, and not from the sources of public information we get. What do we know exactly? We know that Walt Whitman Rostow is a fool. We know that Dean Rusk is a clerk. We know that Mr. Nixon is not really very much worse than the people who preceded him (which is a sufficient judgement on them), and so on. We know all these things not because anyone told us but because events have explained them to us. And it is this explanation that people are looking for.[8]

One does not have to share Kempton's specific substantive judgments to realize that he has managed to capture one of the basic features of our naive prejudices about the world. That is, in our daily concerns with politics, love, sex, friendship, children, making a living, playing games, and virtually everything else of any importance, we rarely if ever evaluate practical information according to the canons of scientific validity. Rather, we seek various "cues" by which we can grasp an intuitive understanding of the idiom, the style, the manner of speaking, the community of sentiments we desire to support or denigrate.

If this understanding about language use in daily life is correct and there does indeed exist an irreducible rhetorical element in all human communications, there appear to be important implications of this for social science objectivity. This seems to call on us to stress the importance of independent checks on the processes and products of research. Independent checks are not the same as institutionalized controls. Driven by a lust for organization, scientists have already created bureaucratic nightmares of institutional controls, and these have been shown to be partly responsible for shackling the potential creativity of the sociological imagination. There are several different levels of independent checks we can insist on to promote our common interests in objective knowledge. One has been discussed in Chapter 6. It is that of the interactions between the observer and his sociological friends, associates, and so forth. A social researcher typically moves back and forth between the realities of the social settings being studied and those of his sociological colleagues, and this "schizophrenic" existence may serve as an important check on whether he is achieving an empathetic rather than a sympathetic understanding in the research. This kind of independent check does not carry with it any foolproof guarantee. It deserves to be taken seriously, however. It does point out the collective responsibilities of our enterprise.

A second level at which we can insist on an independent check is that of the research inquiry itself. Various procedures may be employed to check out the research findings either with the members in the setting or with other knowledgeable individuals. This is commonly referred to as the members' test of validity. For example, if one has studied a setting that is, or has a potential to become, highly politicized, then it is unlikely the use of any members' test will prove useful or illuminating. Any such procedures must always be utilized with the understanding that this checking-out situation potentially constitutes a new and different type of situation. In my investigations of welfare activities, virtually all the written reports and analyses were reviewed by trusted intimates. Two of my close friends who conducted field researches of a psychiatric screening facility at approximately the same time used different verification checks for their observations. One decided to check out her observations by assuming the role of one of the psychiatric screening workers to see if it was possible to reproduce in practice what had been understood on the basis of the research.[9] Another researcher constructed a procedural protocol consisting of an elaborate listing of all the contingent possibilities of psychiatric screening work. He then used this protocol to "predict" the outcome of the screening interviews prior to the actual screening decisions of the psychiatric workers.[10] These are only a few of the possibilities for independently checking out research observations.[11] There are undoubtedly many others which could be used.

In the final analysis, evaluations of the objectivity of social science knowledge depend on our ongoing assessments of our researches in terms of our changing understandings of the fundamental properties of human interaction and communications and on our judgments about the extent to which our scientific understandings are useful for realizing the practical goals of sociology, the solutions of social problems. C. Wright Mills may have played an important role in inspiring a generation of sociologists to return to a classical sociological tradition which was "so often wrong, and yet remain[s] so great." [12] But the time has come to cut through this rhetorical nonsense, to put these sociological traditions to the test of everyday praxis. We must recognize that Max Weber was correct in seeing that at least one of the dimensions of social science objectivity is a moral one. At the most basic level, it is a question of our candor with ourselves and others and, beyond that, of our principled commitments to a theoretical understanding. The ultimate foundations of a truthful understanding of our social existence are our everyday, common-sense experiences as members of society and not a tradition which is considered "great" but is wrong.

NOTES

1. Egon Bittner, "Objectivity and Realism in Sociology," in George Psathas, ed., *Phenomenological Sociology*. New York: John Wiley, forthcoming.
2. Materials on the Lewis–Redfield dispute may be found in the following sources: Robert Redfield, *Tepoztlan, a Mexican Village,* Chicago: The University of Chicago Press, 1930; *The Primitive World and Its Transformations,* Ithaca, N.Y.: Cornell University Press, 1953, especially pp. 155–7; and *The Little Community,* Chicago: The University of Chicago Press, 1955, especially pp.

133–6. Also see Oscar Lewis, *Life in a Mexican Village: Tepoztlan Restudied*. Urbana: The University of Illinois Press, 1951, especially pp. 428–48. For other references to the phenomenon of investigators redefining their researches after the fact, the reader is referred to the works cited in note 21 of Chapter 7.

3. See Joseph G. Weis, "Dialogue with David Matza," *Issues in Criminology*, 6, 1 (Winter 1971): 35–53.

4. See Richard A. Berk and Joseph M. Adams, "Establishing Rapport with Deviant Groups," *Social Problems*, 18 (Summer 1970): 102–17.

5. See Thomas Robbins, Dick Anthony, and Thomas Curtis, "The Limits of Symbolic Realism," *Journal for the Scientific Study of Religion*, 12 (September 1973): 259–73.

6. On the distinction between introspection and self-observation, I have benefited greatly from my discussions with Jack Douglas. See his "Existential Sociology," unpublished manuscript, 1974.

7. See Aron Gurwitsch, *Studies in Phenomenology and Psychology*. Evanston, Ill.: Northwestern University Press, 1956.

8. David Gelman and Beverly Kempton, "The Trouble with Newspapers: An Interview with Murray Kempton," *The Washington Monthly*, 1 (April 1969): 26.

9. The reference is to field research conducted by Rochelle Kern Daniels, which is described in greater detail in her unpublished paper "Experiences as a Participant Observer in Two Units of a Community Mental Health Center," Department of Sociology, University of California, San Diego, July 1972. Interestingly, I was afforded the opportunity to assume the role of a social worker for the purposes of making visits to the homes of welfare clients, but declined on what I then saw as ethical grounds. Later, having had additional opportunities to reflect on my "methodological Puritanism" (at least in this respect), and having had further discussions and arguments about this with Rochelle Daniels and John Anderson, I reached the inescapable conclusion that there existed no available evidence to determine the effectiveness of either practice.

10. The reference is to field research conducted by John P. Anderson, which is reported in greater detail in his "Decision Making in a

Public Psychiatric Screening Agency,'' unpublished Ph.D. dissertation, Department of Social Relations, Harvard University, 1972.

11. One might be tempted to think of such independent checks as relatively unimportant until one recalls that some observers have reported that when a research project had progressed to the reporting stage, there was a desire to analyze some aspects of the setting about which no data had been collected, and it was "too late . . . to go back to the field." How such dilemmas are actually resolved remains a mystery. The quoted phrase is from Blanche Geer, "Studying a College," p. 98 in Robert W. Habenstein, ed., *Pathways to Data*. Chicago: Aldine, 1970.

12. The reference is to Mills's "Introduction: The Classic Tradition," pp. 1–17 in C. Wright Mills, ed., *Images of Man*. New York: George Braziller, 1960, especially p. 3.

Index